Making Sense of Hebrews

Making Sense of Hebrews: Illustrating the Need to Rightly Divide the Word of Truth
Copyright © 2024 by Jose E. Hernandez

Published in the United States of America

Library of Congress Control Number: 2024905801
ISBN   Paperback: 979-8-89091-697-6
ISBN   eBook: 979-8-89091-698-3

All rights reserved. No part of this publication may be reproduced, stored in a retrieval system or transmitted in any way by any means, electronic, mechanical, photocopy, recording or otherwise without the prior permission of the author except as provided by USA copyright law.

The opinions expressed by the author are not necessarily those of ReadersMagnet, LLC.

ReadersMagnet, LLC
10620 Treena Street, Suite 230 | San Diego, California, 92131 USA
1.619. 354. 2643 | www.readersmagnet.com

Book design copyright © 2024 by ReadersMagnet, LLC. All rights reserved.

Cover design by Tifanny Curaza
Interior design by Don De Guzman

Making Sense of Hebrews

Illustrating the Need to Rightly Divide The Word of Truth

Jose E. Hernandez

Dedication

To my wife and sons

The Gospel of the Grace of God

1) Admit you are a sinner

"As it is written, There is none righteous, no, not one:" Rom 3:10

"For all have sinned, and come short of the glory of God" Rom 3:23

"Only **acknowledge thine iniquity**, that thou hast transgressed against the LORD thy God..." Jer. 3:13a

2) Recognize that the outcome of your sin is death

"For the wages of sin is death..." Rom 6:23

"...death passed upon all men, for that all have sinned" Rom 5:12b

3) Believe that "Christ died for our sins" and rose again.

"But God commendeth his love toward us, in that, while we were yet sinners, Christ died for us." Rom 5:8

"...**Christ died for our sins** according to the scriptures" 1Cor 15:3

"...by the grace of God should taste death for every man." Heb. 2:9

4) God grants the gift of eternal life to those believing.

"...gift of God is eternal life through Jesus Christ our Lord." Rom 6:23

"...it is the gift of God: Not of works..." Eph. 2:8, 9

5) Believe and receive the gift today – don't reject it!

"...we beg you on behalf of Christ, be reconciled to God." 2Cor. 5:20 nasb

"...now is THE ACCEPTABLE TIME, behold, now is "THE DAY OF SALVATION" 2Cor. 6:2 nasb

Believe that Christ "...was delivered for our offences, and was raised again for our justification." Rom 4:25

And you will be declared righteous.

Contents

Dedication 4
The Gospel of the Grace of God 5
Preface 9
Hebrews in 155 Words 13

Chapter 1:   Jerusalem, Paul and Acts 15
Chapter 2:   Floater 22
Chapter 3:   Overview 29
Chapter 4:   "But Now We See Not" 37
Chapter 5:   "The Words Which Thou Gavest Me" 48
Chapter 6:   Melchisedec 58
Chapter 7:   Their God – My People 67
Chapter 8:   Blood 101 80
Chapter 9:   "A better covenant" 91
Chapter 10: Perfection 102
Chapter 11: "the profession of our faith" 120
Chapter 12: Unfinished Business 131
Chapter 13: Odds and Ends 137

Appendix – The Rest of God 147

Unless otherwise indicated, all Scriptures are from the King James Version

Scripture quotations marked **ESV** are from the English Standard Version

Scripture quotations marked **NASB** are from the New American Standard Bible

Scripture quotations marked **NIV** are from the New International Version

Scripture quotations marked **BLB** are from the Berean Literal Bible

Scripture quotations marked **BSB** are from the Berean Study Bible

Scripture quotations marked **YLT** are from Young's Literal Translation

Scripture quotations marked **NKJV** are from the New King James Version

Scripture quotations marked **RSV** are from the Revised Standard Version

Scripture quotations marked **HCS** are from the Holman Christian Standard

Preface

Hebrews is perhaps the most challenging book to understand in the New Testament. It's not that its message is difficult – it is fairly forthright. It's that it is a "floater" having minimal ties to any other New Testament book. This causes some anxiety and, unfortunately, some see it as an opportunity to make it agree with and promote their theology or agenda.

We are not told who wrote it or to whom it was addressed. We have very sketchy data regarding the date it was written. And we have little information from where it was written and where it ended up. In short, we have scant information concerning who, when, where and how. But, we have plenty of what and why!

The what and why are laid out in a straightforward, logical sequence using very little in terms of metaphors and proverbs. There are no deep meanings to decipher and, with the exception of Chapter 11, Moses and Christ are the prominent characters in the main chapters - with Abraham and Melchisedec making a short appearance in Chapters 5 through 7.

Hebrews is also unique in that it attributes to Christ certain titles which are absent in all the other books of the Bible. Nowhere, except for Hebrews, is Christ ever referred to as a priest – much less a high priest. Closely related, is the name Melchisedec. It is found once in Genesis, once in Psalms and nine times in Hebrews. I still find that fact remarkable. I imagine that on that fact alone, Hebrews was approved by some committee as belonging to Scripture.

Hebrews gradually reveals the substance upon which the shadow religion of Judaism was constructed. The epistle strongly relies upon the reader's familiarity of Israel's ceremonial law - the sacrifices, the tabernacle, the ordinances of divine service and, finally, the high priest – in order to unfold the specifics and benefits of the substance. It employs comparison/contrast and uses well known Old Testament characters such as angels, Moses, David, Joshua and Abraham to logically and step-by-step bring the substance into full view.

Preface

And it does this, all the while, having reminded the reader in the very first lines that Christ "Hath in these last days spoken unto us". Christ spoke as The Prophet. The readers are sharply warned in Chapters 3 and 4 to "hear his voice" reminding them of the dire consequences their unbelieving ancestors bore – "whose carcases fell in the wilderness". And in Chapter 12, the epistle draws to a close with the same emphasis of Christ speaking.

> "See that ye refuse not him that speaketh. For if they escaped not who refused him that spake on earth, much more shall not we escape, if we turn away from him that speaketh from heaven:" Heb 12:25

The goal of Hebrews was to encourage its original readers, those who had believed Jesus of Nazareth was indeed Israel's Messiah, to continue toward the one and only high priest: Christ Jesus. Thus, the believing Israelite was encouraged to confidently "draw near *[to God]* with a true heart" knowing "he is faithful that promised". Though "illuminated" in "the former days" and "partakers of the heavenly calling", they were dangerously close to relapsing to the shadows of the Old Covenant.

In addition to the use of familiar Old Testament characters, the epistle methodically introduces certain words and concepts throughout its pages in order to obtain its goal. We will discuss some of these words at length. However, it is very beneficial to keep an eye on the constellation of key words found in the final chapters while diving into the specifics. Chief among these key words are: high priest, testament/covenant and mediator.

Like many commentaries before, we hold that the original readers were converts. The majority of commentaries have the original readers converting from Judaism to Christianity; specifically, the Body of Christ. However, we differ in that we believe they were converted from the shadows of the Old Covenant to the substance: "the high priest Christ Jesus as the mediator of the New Covenant". Which, in our view, is not the same as "the body *[of Christ]*, the church" as defined in Paul's epistles. We believe the original readers were aligned doctrinally with the believers at Pentecost. Throughout the commentary we will provide scriptural support for this view.

Preface

But for now, we point out that our view helps to clarify two major inconsistencies. These inconsistencies primarily concern today's believers and their association with the Law and eternal security. We hold that members of the Body of Christ have died with Christ and to the Law. We have been sealed and thus have eternal security. But in stark contrast, there is not the slightest indication that the original recipients of the Hebrew epistle had died with Christ or to the Law. And there are ample verses/passages which strongly suggest they did not have eternal security. We will elaborate on these positions as the book unfolds.

These inconsistencies disappear when we understand that, while both groups [the original Hebrew readers and members of the Body of Christ] are "believers", they represent two distinct programs of God. The author's 2nd book – DIED WITH CHRIST – addresses this subject in detail. Unlike phraseology found in Paul's epistles, the Hebrew epistle **never** tells or reminds its original recipients they "died with Christ" (Rom 6:3, 4, 8; Col 2:20). Nor are they ever reminded that they "died to the Law" (Rom 7:4, 6; Gal 2:19). The fact is they were not reminded they died with anybody because they never did. Paul used that phraseology often in his epistles to get wayward members of the Body of Christ back to God. It seems to us that if these Hebrew readers had been members of the Body of Christ, reminding them they had died with Christ **and to the Law** would have quickly resolved the whole issue!

Many qualified commentators begin by devoting a chapter or two "proving" that the author was Paul. Then, they explain certain passages of Hebrews from a Pauline viewpoint. This is circular reasoning. Paul may have been the author, but the fact is the Holy Spirit never put that in writing. "But look at this verse and that passage; the author just has to be Paul" – a persistent position.

One popular association to Paul is the assertion by many that Peter's words: "...our beloved brother Paul...hath written unto you" in 2Pet 3:15b is a strong reference to the book of Hebrews. But, surprisingly, the subject of 2Pet 3:15, "the longsuffering of our Lord is salvation", is practically non-existent in the pages of Hebrews. We will elaborate on this in some detail.

Preface

We have chosen to present this Hebrew commentary based solely on the information found in its pages and the Scriptures. Our aim is to understand the context primarily from the letter alone. And though we make an occasional remark on authorship, it is not our intent to favor one or the other. We pray that it will, nonetheless, edify and bless our readers.

Ernie
March/2024

Hebrews in 155 Words

The jist of Hebrews is God's promise to Israel; that of realizing the New Covenant of Jeremiah 31. God had put in place His high priest (for the reconciliation of sins) and The Prophet (to "hear his voice") as divine offices whereby the partakers would find guidance, encouragement, mercy and grace "in time of need" as they journeyed in the race "set before us".

However, the partakers were wavering and returning to the Levitical system. To counter this, the author spends 30-40% of the epistle demonstrating the superiority of the priesthood of Christ over the lesser Levitical priesthood. The message is clear: those who do not "hold fast the profession of our faith" – with immediate attention upon Jesus Christ as God's high priest – will not take part in the New Covenant.

Hebrews concerns itself with the fulfillment of God's prophetic promises made to Israel. It has limited impact regarding the "mystery among the Gentiles".

CHAPTER 1

Jerusalem, Paul and Acts

QuickTake:

> An understanding of the landscape of Acts is needful to grasp the message of Hebrews. Acts begins with the familiar cast found in the Gospels and records the phenomenal growth of the "little flock". However, the direction takes an unexpected turn with the rise of an unknown - Saul of Tarsus, also Paul. And though there are overlapping chapters between the Jerusalem leadership and Paul, the conclusions are still not clear to many.
>
> With the latter chapters of Acts focusing on Paul, the influence of Jerusalem and Judaism upon the larger Jewish community takes a backseat. However, Paul's visits to Jerusalem (Acts 15 and 21) demonstrated their influence had not lost much ground, if any, to the rapidly growing Mystery program.

Since Israel had been cast away well before Romans 11, the evangelization of the early-Acts prophetic promises regarding the restoration of David's Jerusalem-centered throne was in a significant decline. Peter and the rest of the Twelve faded from the scriptural scene by Acts 15 and Paul became the main character. With the raising up of Paul, God was advancing the mystery resulting in miraculous growth in many regions outside Judaea and Jerusalem.

Yet, at Pentecost, a tremendous seed had been sown, which quickly grew and blossomed from a handful to thousands – the "little flock". We ask: What happened to the "little flock"? These were the thousands who believed and were "added to the Lord" at Pentecost (Acts 2:41, 47; 4:4; 5:14-16). Acts 2:9-11 lists over 15 regions represented in Jerusalem the day the Holy Spirit filled the disciples.

These, no doubt, returned home to their local circles and spread the exciting news of the risen Messiah ready to restore David's throne to prominence. These small, local circles consisted of Pentecostal believers making up part of the larger Jewish community. In this book, we refer to these outside-of-Jerusalem believers as Partakers – taken from Heb 3:1. That the Partakers and the "little flock" are one and the same cannot be supported. Nevertheless, Heb 2:1-4 tells us they were doctrinally aligned, having the fulfillment of Israel's prophetic promises as their hope.

The Authority and Leadership of Jerusalem

But even though the nation of Israel had been cast away, we submit that, in the eyes of the Jewish community at large, the authority and leadership of the Jerusalem elders had not diminished in the time period of Acts. Note the following:

1) Jews "out of every nation under heaven" continued to make yearly pilgrimages to Jerusalem (Acts 12:3; 20:16; 21:20, 27; 24:18).
2) The book of Acts referred to the leadership in Jerusalem as "elders" (Acts 11:30; 15:2, 4, 6, 22, 23; 16:4; 21:18).
3) Though Paul and the Jerusalem leadership agreed to certain parameters upon their respective ministries (Acts 15/Gal 2), those details were not publicly announced.
4) The only public, tangible outcome from the Acts 15/Gal 2 meeting was an authoritative letter from the Jerusalem leadership addressed to the Gentiles.
5) In the eyes of those with whom Paul met, the fact that he carried that letter on his person validated the authority of the Jerusalem leadership.

And finally, as will be demonstrated below, Paul's visits to Jerusalem confirmed the uninterrupted standing of the Jerusalem leadership to both Jewish and Gentile communities at large.

Popular Notions

Now Hebrews is generally agreed to have been penned in the latter part of Acts – during Paul's most active years. Couple this with the popular notions that the church, the Body of Christ started at Pentecost and that Paul wrote Hebrews, the assumption is made that the Hebrews epistle can only contain "Body truth".

Their thinking goes something like this:

> "Starting at Pentecost with the birth of the church, the Body of Christ, the gospel of grace quickly proliferated. First in and around Jerusalem; but then quickly into Asia and Europe. The gospel of Israel's kingdom had been superseded. The gospel of the grace of God was the only message actively disseminated/circulated during the book of Acts. So at the time Hebrews was written (late Acts) the grace gospel had been firmly established by Paul and his coworkers. Therefore, since Paul wrote Hebrews, he undoubtedly would write about the gospel of the grace of God – that goes without saying!"

And while that argument may sound plausible, we believe the assumption has little scriptural support. Our position is based on Paul's visits to Jerusalem in Acts 15 and Acts 21. We have touched on this briefly, but we hold that the outcomes of these meetings strengthened the public perception (whether real or not) that:

(1) The leadership in Jerusalem was fully intact.
(2) Their spiritual authority had not faded.
(3) Therefore Israelites, far and near, could look toward this established leadership for guidance and direction.

The outcomes were:
1) Acts 15 - The Jerusalem meeting resulted in a **letter** penned by the Jerusalem leadership. Paul took a copy of that letter and "delivered them the decrees" as he travelled through cities outside of Judaea and Jerusalem.

2) Acts 21 - Paul agreed to James's instructions in Acts 21:23, 24. He **participated in animal offerings** in the temple in Jerusalem. This occurred during Pentecost.

We touch on their significance below.

Background

The Apostles, whose understanding of the scriptures had been opened (Luke 24:45) and had listened to the risen Christ speak of the "things pertaining to the kingdom of God" (Acts 1:3), knew full well the sequence of events upon the prophetic horizon. Peter demonstrated this divine knowledge quoting three passages in rapid succession at Pentecost – Joel 2, Psa 16 and Psa 110. But, those prophetic milestones never occurred. There was no great tribulation. The Man of Sin did not appear on the scene. Daniel's vision progressed no further than the 69th week. So what happened? This question was surely raised by the Pentecostal believers – the "little flock". What had happened to their hope?

God's "mystery among the gentiles" happened. Approximately 25 years after the cross, Paul informed the Romans that Israel had been cast away – it had occurred years before. God had placed Israel's prophetic program on hold while the mystery advanced. But note, Rom 11:25-27 clearly reminds us that this was a temporary postponement. God had not forgotten His promises to the Twelve Tribes of Israel.

> "For I would not, brethren, that ye should be ignorant of this mystery, lest ye should be wise in your own conceits; that blindness in part is happened to Israel, until the fulness of the Gentiles be come in.
>
> And so all Israel shall be saved: as it is written, There shall come out of Sion the Deliverer, and shall turn away ungodliness from Jacob:
>
> For this is my covenant unto them, when I shall take away their sins." Rom 11:25-27

This postponement is nearing almost 2000 years.

We ask: Did God tell Paul or Peter or anybody else how long the postponement would last? No - that information is not found in the Bible. However, some Pauline statements suggest that the Apostle may have thought God's mystery would end shortly (Acts 20:24; Rom 13:11, 12; 16:20; 1Cor 7:29; 1Ths 4:15). Of course, there is no way of knowing what Paul actually thought. Because we have acclimated to the 2000-year postponement, it is "normal" to us. And we imperceptibly assume those in the Acts time period also thought the mystery was the new "business as usual" – that it would last a long time. But that assumption is groundless.

I've heard pastors say something like "the time is short, now is the day of salvation. We are not promised tomorrow. It could end tonight" - to which we agree. But, that same thinking also applied during Paul's time period. I would think, but can't prove, that the Apostle was asked many times "how long will it last?"

The Letter

Early on in the Acts narrative, the Lord had commanded a young Saul to depart from Jerusalem, sending him "far hence unto the Gentiles". And as the mystery program prospered in many areas outside Jerusalem, Paul was given responsibility and authority over the gentile churches (1Cor 4:17; 7:17; Titus 1:5). However, Paul had no jurisdiction over the church in Jerusalem. Indeed, he had been told to leave Jerusalem (Acts 22:18). A study of Paul's meetings with the elders of Jerusalem in Acts 15 and Acts 21 demonstrates that James and the elders were clearly in charge. And, by displaying their authority, the Jerusalem leadership demonstrated that Judaism was very much alive. Undeniably, Gal 4:25 tells us they were in bondage. Nevertheless, that did not undermine their influence.

The letter issued by "The apostles and elders and brethren" in Acts 15 disclosed they were the decision makers. The recognition of the letter by others only promoted the authority of the Jerusalem leadership. Specifically, the rejoicing by the gentiles upon receiving the letter (Acts

15:31) and Paul's deliverance of "the decrees" (Acts 16:4) indicated an acknowledgment of the authority of the Jerusalem church.

The fact that the Apostle of the Gentiles, while traveling through regions far from Jerusalem, placed value upon a letter written by the leadership of the Jerusalem church, demonstrated to the Jewish and Gentile communities in those regions that Paul recognized their authority.

An Offering in Jerusalem

Approximately 8 to 10 years after Acts 15, Paul entered Jerusalem in Acts 21:17 and didn't waste any time meeting with "James; and all the elders". After some discussion, James directed Paul to pay the charges for some Mosaic purification offerings - and Paul agreed. Admittedly, Paul's active participation in the purification offerings is perplexing. Nevertheless, it publically gave the perception that the Jerusalem leadership had not lost any of its position of authority relative to the Apostle of the Gentiles. Indeed, it may have been elevated in the eyes of some. The communities at large would reasonably perceive, reinforced by Paul's temple ceremonial actions in Jerusalem, that Jerusalem's influence and authority over him was very real. This may not have been Paul's intent. But, that is the obvious conclusion from Paul's Jerusalem visit.

Take it Back Home

Now since Paul's temple offerings occurred during Pentecost (Acts 20:16), many Jews from foreign cities were visiting Jerusalem. And since "all the city was moved" (Acts 21:30) by Paul's presence in the temple, the foreign visitors had certainly heard of the turmoil because "all Jerusalem was in an uproar" (Acts 21:31). Upon returning to their respective countries, they would naturally have shared the news of Paul's heated and divisive offerings in Jerusalem – all together, that was big news!

This news would gradually filter down to the believers in Hebrews – the Partakers. Because Paul's two Jerusalem visits only elevated the position of the Jerusalem church in the eyes of the Hebrews, there was no big incentive to gravitate away from Judaism to the Mystery. Why? Because in their eyes, Judaism and the Jerusalem leadership were still active and intact. So, even though they acknowledged the "mystery among the gentiles" (or at least knew about it), it could end at any time. And if so, God would revert back to Israel and Jerusalem to fulfill His promises. The believers in Hebrews were not deterred by this undocumented mystery program. God was a God of promises. And, in contrast to the mystery, His promises toward Israel had been clearly documented for hundreds of years – it was in writing! They would hold on to their prophetic hope – the establishment of the New Covenant – knowing that God always keeps His promises.

A Final Thought

As noted earlier, Christ had told Paul to "get thee quickly out of Jerusalem" (Acts 22:18). And in his last recorded journey to Jerusalem, he was warned not to go there (Acts 20:23; 21:4, 11, 12). Clearly, Jerusalem was "off limits" to Paul. The "apostles, and elders and brethren" (Acts 15:23) were their own church independent of Paul's ministry – and his was independent of theirs. This was further demonstrated by the "right hands of fellowship" of Gal 2:9. Thus, even though God's mystery program was expanding far and wide, we conclude that, though the nation of Israel had been cast away, the influence of the Jerusalem leadership had not diminished in regions far from David's city. Jerusalem's influence remained intact – at least through the book of Acts.

We can see how keeping Jerusalem independent and influential throughout the book of Acts would have promoted the idea that the Mystery was perhaps a short-term event. And keeping distance between Jerusalem and Paul helped bolster that perception.

CHAPTER 2

Floater

QuickTake:

> In this chapter we will look at how Hebrews fits in with the other 25 New Testament books. The letter is examined for any tangible data regarding the date, authorship, readership and content. We are particularly interested in the readers to whom Hebrews was written. To avoid confusion with today's readership, we will use the term Partakers (Heb 3:1) to identify those to whom Hebrews was originally addressed.

Date

Though the date Hebrews was written is not clear-cut, there are certain markers which help us get a rough idea. It's a given the author wrote the letter sometime after the events of Pentecost.

> "How shall we escape, if we neglect so great salvation; which at the first began to be spoken by the Lord, and was confirmed unto us by them that heard him;
>
> God also bearing them witness, both with signs and wonders, and with divers miracles, and gifts of the Holy Ghost, according to his own will?" Heb 2:3, 4

But a period of time had elapsed since Pentecost. The author had expectations on their spiritual maturity. Unfortunately, it wasn't where it should be. They had regressed.

> "For when for the time ye ought to be teachers, ye have need that one teach you again which be the first principles of the

oracles of God; and are become such as have need of milk, and not of strong meat." Heb 5:12

This lapse of time agrees with a passage in the 10th Chapter, in which the author reminded them of the "former days".

> "But call to remembrance the former days, in which, after ye were illuminated, ye endured a great fight of afflictions;"
>
> Partly, whilst ye were made a gazingstock both by reproaches and afflictions; and partly, whilst ye became companions of them that were so used.
>
> For ye had compassion of me in my bonds, and took joyfully the spoiling of your goods, knowing in yourselves that ye have in heaven a better and an enduring substance." Heb 10:32-34

Those who believe Paul wrote Hebrews suggest the "my bonds" of v.34 refers to his 2-year imprisonment of Acts 24:23-27 in Caesarea. That would indicate the date of the letter occurred after the major events regarding Paul found in the book of Acts.

However, it should be noted that in many Greek texts, the term "my bonds" does not appear in Heb 10:34. For example the ESV reads:

> "For you had compassion on those in prison, and you joyfully accepted the plundering of your property, since you knew that you yourselves had a better possession and an abiding one." Heb 10:34 (ESV)

The reference to Italy in the closing lines of Hebrews

> "Salute all them that have the rule over you, and all the saints. They of Italy salute you." Heb 13:24

suggests the letter was written by Paul while in Rome. Yet, some commentators suggest that Paul may not have been in Italy, but was surrounded by a group of Italian believers known to the Partakers.

The most specific piece of information occurs in Heb 13:23.

> "Know ye that our brother Timothy is set at liberty; with whom, if he come shortly, I will see you." Heb 13:23

If this Timothy is Paul's Timothy (a reasonable assumption), then the letter was written well past Acts 16. The first mention of Timothy, by name, is found in Acts 16:1, shortly after Paul embarked on his second apostolic journey (approximately 51 AD). This would place the date, at its earliest, sometime toward the latter part of Acts.

One can see that making hard conclusions regarding the exact date of the epistle is difficult.

Authorship - Readership

Each verse was examined, looking for any indication, no matter how slight, that would give insight regarding the identity of the author or the Partakers. The list below summarizes the search:

Heb 2:3 – "…confirmed unto us by them that heard him"
Heb 2:5 – "…the world to come, whereof we speak"
Heb 3:1 – "…holy brethren, partakers of the heavenly calling…"
Heb 5:11 – "…ye are dull of hearing."
Heb 5:12 – "…ye ought to be teachers…"
Heb 5:12 – "…such as have need of milk, and not of strong meat"
Heb 6:10 – "…your work and labour of love…"
Heb 6:10 – "…ye have shewed toward his name…"
Heb 6:10 – "…ye have ministered to the saints, and do minister"
Heb 6:18 – "…we…who have fled for refuge…"
Heb 10:25 – "…as the manner of some…"
Heb 10:32 – "…former days…ye were illuminated…"
Heb 10:32 – "…endured a great fight of afflictions"

Heb 10:33 – "…ye were made a gazingstock…"
Heb 10:33 – "…ye became companions…"
Heb 10:34 – "…ye had compassion of me in my bonds…"
Heb 10:34 – "…took joyfully the spoiling of your goods…"
Heb 12:5 – "…ye have forgotten the exhortation…"
Heb 13:7 – "Remember them which have the rule over you…"
Heb 13:17 – "Obey them that have the rule over you…"
Heb 13:19 – "…that I may be restored to you the sooner"
Heb 13:22 – "…I have written a letter unto you…"
Heb 13:23 – "…brother Timothy is set at liberty…"
Heb 13:23 – "…if he come shortly, I will see you"
Heb 13:24 – "…They of Italy salute you"

From the list, one can see that nothing specific regarding identity is revealed. These general descriptions could readily apply to any one of many churches. However, four verses at the close of the epistle may provide some additional insight regarding the relationship between the author and the Partakers.

> "Remember them which have the rule over you, who have spoken unto you the word of God: whose faith follow, considering the end of their conversation." Heb 13:7

> "Obey them that have the rule over you, and submit yourselves: for they watch for your souls, as they that must give account, that they may do it with joy, and not with grief: for that is unprofitable for you." Heb 13:17

> "But I beseech you the rather to do this, that I may be restored to you the sooner." Heb 13:19

> "Salute all them that have the rule over you, and all the saints. They of Italy salute you." Heb 13:24

Verses 13:7, 17 and 24 indicate that the author was concerned about maintaining a structured, orderly assembly. Thrice, he uses the phrase "rule over you". His admonition was "Remember them", "Obey them" and "Salute all them". Also, Heb 13:19 indicates the author had a personal connection to his readers and was looking forward to joining them soon; to be "restored to you *[plural]* the sooner." Therefore, it appears that Hebrews may have been written to one specific assembly; rather than to an entire nation spanning different countries as the name "Hebrews" may suggest. We are reminded that even the word "Hebrews" is not found in the text.

Thus far, not much has been uncovered which would link this epistle to the rest of the New Testament. We don't know when it was written. We don't know with absolute certainty who wrote it. We don't know to whom it was addressed. We don't know what countries were involved. But we have an idea that, perhaps, it was written toward the end of the book of Acts.

Contents

Let's examine the contents for additional light. Surprising to many, the purpose of the letter is fairly straightforward. Its main emphasis is a contrast of two priesthoods. One is the shadow system of the Levitical system and the other is the substance of Jesus Christ, His priestly office and His mediation of the New Covenant found in the book of Jeremiah. The Partakers, previously illuminated and who had endured afflictions and loss of property for the "new and living way", were wavering and possibly regressing back to the shadows. The author used the adjective "better" thirteen times throughout the letter to convince/exhort the Partakers to stay the course.

All the Old Testament characters referred to in Hebrews would be familiar to the Partakers. However, the name Melchizedec would likely be foreign to even the scribes of the day, seeing that it occurred only twice outside the book of Hebrews. I don't doubt that the detailed explanation and revelation given to this name found in the book of Hebrews secured it a place in the sacred scripture. For without Hebrews, we wouldn't have a clue what significance Melchizedec played in God's redemption plan. Hebrews and Hebrews alone, revealed the details of the priesthood of Jesus Christ and its critical impact on the New Covenant as it relates to the House of Israel.

As far as content is concerned, a rough summary is provided below:

- Christ's deity & sufferings
- Exhortation and warning
- Doctrine – limits of the Levitical priesthood
- The better priesthood of Christ
- Application
- Mediator of the New Covenant
- Heroes of Faith
- Mount Sion
- Closing encouragements

The gist of Hebrews is Christ as high priest and as the mediator of the New Covenant. This is at the heart of Hebrews. It is because of His priesthood, that Christ has the authority to be the mediator of the New Covenant. The establishment of the New Covenant is the goal of God's prophetic program to Israel. The priesthood of Jesus Christ is a necessary precursor by which the New Testament of Jeremiah 31:31-34 will be established. Israel's prophetic program could not be fulfilled by the Levitical priesthood which was weak and unprofitable. A perfect, everlasting priesthood was required.

Key Words

There are certain words that are key in any epistle in that they occur more frequently than other words or they occur only in that letter. Hebrews has its share of keywords such as Promise, Testament/Covenant, Enter, Rest and Better. However, Priest (Strongs# 2409), High Priest (Strongs# 749), and Priesthood (Strongs# 2420) have the most occurrences of all the keywords and are unique to Hebrews. These keywords pertaining to Jesus Christ clearly do not occur in the writings of Paul, Peter, James, John or Jude. His priesthood is never declared or revealed in those epistles.

This is why it is difficult to link Hebrews to other New Testament writings. In other writings, the priesthood of Jesus Christ is non-existent. While in Hebrews, it's the core issue. It's that black and white. There are no gray areas of overlap. True, one will find the words "intercession" and "the new testament" in Paul's writings:

> "Who is he that condemneth? It is Christ that died, yea rather, that is risen again, who is even at the right hand of God, who also maketh intercession for us." Rom 8:34

> "After the same manner also he took the cup, when he had supped, saying, This cup is the new testament in my blood: this do ye, as oft as ye drink it, in remembrance of me." 1Cor 11:25

> "Who also hath made us able ministers of the new testament; not of the letter, but of the spirit: for the letter killeth, but the spirit giveth life." 2Cor 3:6

Some believe these verses provide such a link. It is our purpose in writing this commentary, to see if those links are non-existent or have merit. However, we need to keep in mind that the occurrence of certain words in other Bible books, does not automatically mean those books are speaking to the same people, about the same subject. The context must be examined to hopefully make a determination one way or the other.

Conclusion:

1) If "Timothy" in Heb 13:23 is Paul's friend, Hebrews was written after Acts 16.
2) The author was not identified in Hebrews.
3) The Partakers were not identified in Hebrews.
4) The Partakers were wavering or regressing.
5) Jesus Christ is identified as God's High Priest.
6) The word "Hebrews" does not appear in the text.
7) It is not obvious how this letter was given its title.

CHAPTER 3

Overview

QuickTake:

> We examined the background of Hebrews in the previous chapter. In this chapter the intent of the letter is examined by categorizing its chapters. Logically grouping the 13 chapters will give us a better understanding of the overall message.

We grouped the chapters in an indented outline format. But because the outline is best understood by viewing it on a single page, we left the remainder of this page blank. Please proceed to the next page to view the full outline.

Overview

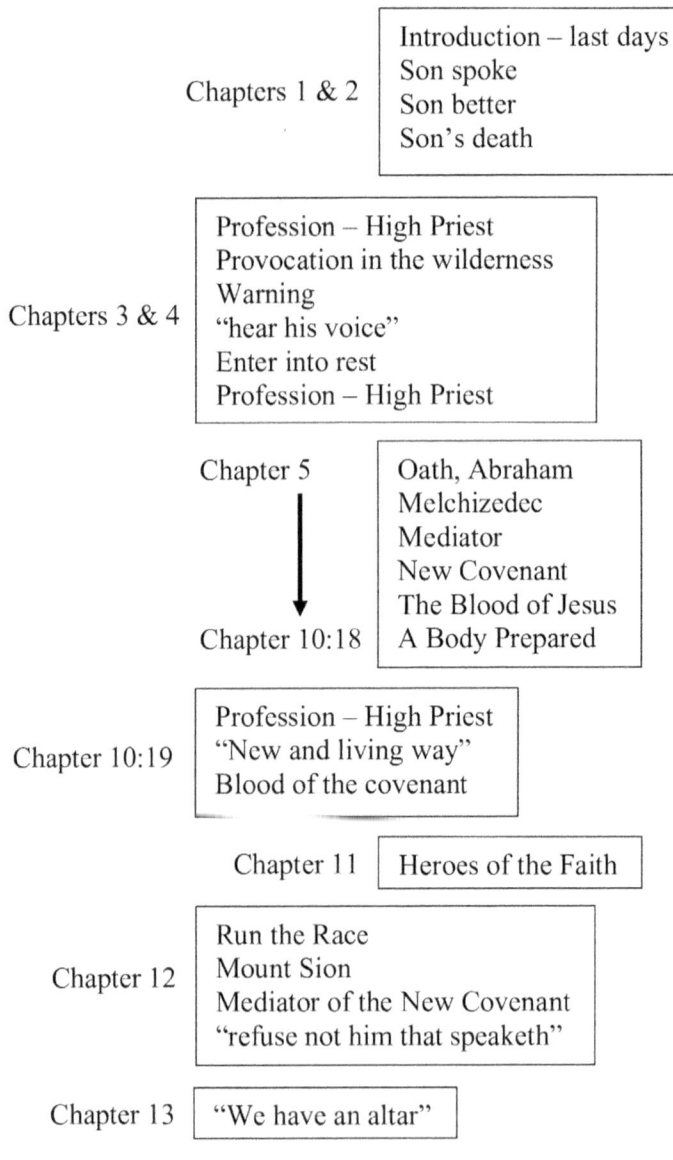

The indented passages (favoring the right side) are generally comprised of historical or doctrinal information intended for the deliberation of the Partakers. These passages are not about the Partakers. They provide Biblical truths. In contrast, the non-indented passages are "speaking" directly to the Partakers. By this, I mean that these passages primarily consist of encouragements and exhortations (Heb 3:13; 10:25; 12:5; 13:22) consistent with what they learned in the indented passages. However, it is not black and white. There are overlaps; but for the most part these chapter groupings hold. We believe the primary purpose of Hebrews is found in these non-indented passages (favoring the left side). First comes knowledge, followed by action in line with that knowledge.

The Non-Indented Passages

If we set the indented passages aside momentarily, the outline appears as such. See next page:

Overview

Chapters 3 & 4	**Profession** – High Priest Provocation in the wilderness Warning "hear his voice" Enter into rest **Profession** – High Priest
Chapter 10:19	**Profession** – High Priest "New and living way" Blood of the covenant
Chapter 12	Run the Race Mount Sion Mediator of the New Covenant "refuse not him that speaketh"
Chapter 13	"We have an altar"

Notice that the word "profession" emerges. Hebrews contains three occurrences of this word. They are:

> "Wherefore, holy brethren, partakers of the heavenly calling, consider the Apostle and **High Priest** of our **profession**, Christ Jesus;" Heb 3:1

> "Seeing then that we have a great **high priest**, that is passed into the heavens, Jesus the Son of God, let us hold fast our **profession**." Heb 4:14

> "And having an **high priest**...Let us hold fast the **profession** of our faith *[hope]* without wavering; (for he is faithful that promised;)" Heb 10:21a, 23

Each occurrence of "profession" is associated with Christ as the High Priest. It was not enough that Christ was the high priest; but that He was the high priest **"of our profession"**. Scriptural facts are of no use if not retained and applied personally. The "hold fast" in the verses above is taken from two Greek words whose meanings are retain, possess, secure with strength or power.

The author exhorted his readers to embrace their "Christ-as-the-High-Priest" profession – and embrace it with all their might. And in order to believe it with conviction, they needed to fully understand it. However, apart from the book of Hebrews, the rest of Scripture provided no information regarding Christ as a high priest. Consequently, the author devoted a sizeable portion of the letter disclosing the details of the priesthood with one objective: Demonstrating the authenticity and superiority of the priesthood of Christ. This sizeable portion is found in the indented passages, which we will address next.

We want to understand, in some depth, what the profession of the "holy brethren" entailed. Chapters 5 and 11 of this book explore it in some detail. It is touched upon in subsequent chapters. Our examination will be somewhat deep, taking us back to the very days Moses led the nation of Israel out of Egypt. The history associated with the readership and their profession will help us to understand the latter chapters of Hebrews, where the emphasis shifts toward the New Covenant.

The Indented Passages

The purpose of the non-indented passages was to encourage the Partakers to "hold fast the profession of our faith", which was strongly tied to the priesthood of Christ. The legitimacy of the priesthood of Christ was developed in the largest indentation, which made up roughly 40% of the letter. This major indentation (refer to the outline on page thirty) is that portion of Hebrews from Heb 5 to Heb 10:18.

Two points justified its length: (1) the New Covenant could not exist without the priesthood of Jesus Christ and (2) The Partakers had to be totally convinced that Christ's priesthood was legitimate, superior and the **only** way to God's Rest. The second point was no easy task because there was not a single verse or passage in the Old Testament which the author could provide as confirmation.

Overview

But that did not stop the Holy Spirit. He enabled the author to pen an ingenious, logical argument using the Old Testament, which demonstrates the depth and width of the Scriptures. This is a lesson for all Biblical students to learn. It illustrates how God uses Scripture to clearly validate a concrete truth by gathering facts from different times, different peoples and different authors. All these different elements converge upon a result which is without question or doubt. It also testifies to the divine authorship of the Scriptures, for men separated from each other by centuries, country, language and background could not have achieved such a purpose with precise results.

This would be analogous to having numerous puzzle parts spanning 2000 years across different countries fitting perfectly together. This could only happen if there were a master puzzle maker!

The keywords found in the major indentation are: Abraham, oath, Melchizedec, high priest, New Testament and promise. The gist of this portion of Hebrews is the basis for the priesthood of Jesus Christ. There is nothing in the Old Testament (or the New Testament for that matter) which gives any indication that God would have another high priest apart from the tribe of Levi with the exception of one verse: Psa 110:4.

> "The LORD hath sworn, and will not repent, Thou art a priest for ever after the order of Melchizedek." Psa 110:4

But even that verse does not identify the "Thou". Furthermore, the verse only refers to priest not high priest and says nothing about Judah. And since this priest was associated with Melchizedec, one could have reasonably assumed it had something to do with the Gentiles since the only other reference to Melchizedec is found in Gen 14:18. That meeting occurred years before the circumcision of Abraham.

Some point to Zech 6:13. But Joshua is the son of Josedech, the high priest, which points to the Levitical priesthood (v.11).

Just as Important

Hebrews also emphasized Christ as The Prophet. But, unlike the priesthood, the emphasis is not concentrated in a large portion of the letter. And because of the considerable attention given to the priesthood, Christ as The Prophet is typically not addressed by most Hebrews commentators. The importance of this office to Israel cannot be overstated. As a reminder, recall The Prophet was on the same level as Moses (Deut 18:15) and would speak the very words of God (Deut 18:18, 19). Furthermore, disobedience of God's words, spoken by The Prophet, would result in God's judgment (Deut 18:19).

All knew The Prophet would appear. However, WHEN? was the unknown. In John 1:21 and 7:40 the people pondered the long-last arrival of The Prophet. And, in Acts 3:22, 23 the Holy Spirit, through Peter, sealed the deal - Jesus Christ was identified as The Prophet.

Christ spoke the very words of God. The verses below demonstrate its importance in Hebrews.

> Heb 1:2 – "in these last days spoken unto us by his Son"
> Heb 2:3 – "spoken by the Lord"
> Heb 3:7, 15; 4:7 – "hear his voice"
> Heb 12:19 – "voice of words"
> Heb 12:25 – "refuse not him that speaketh…from heaven"

Closing the Epistle

The author started winding down the epistle in the latter part of the 10th chapter. From here we find stern exhortations, mixed with reminders of the "better" promises awaiting them. One of the main objectives of the eleventh chapter was to let them know they were not alone. They were walking in the same shoes as notable Old Testament individuals, who

> "…died in faith, not having received the promises…they were strangers and pilgrims on the earth." Heb 11:13

Overview

The last two verses of Chapter 11 provided much hope, for these verses informed the Partakers that they were included in God's grand design.

As the letter of Hebrews advanced in the final chapters, they received a mix of warnings, exhortations and encouragements. They had received a lengthy treatise regarding the priesthood of Christ Jesus, which made up their "profession". In Chapter 11, they received the fellowship and hope from the "heroes of faith".

In the latter chapters, "Patience" and "Endured" are emphasized.

> "Wherefore seeing we also are compassed about with so great a cloud of witnesses, let us lay aside every weight, and the sin which doth so easily beset us, and let us run with patience the race that is set before us," Heb 12:1

Toward the end of the epistle, the Partakers find themselves at a "fork in the road". On the one side, they had the types with all the bells and whistles of the Levitical system. These included the temple, holy days, the sacrifices, the priests and 1500 years of tradition. These are elements which have a strong appeal to the senses. On the other side, they had the reality and truth of the priesthood of Christ. Absent was anything "touchy feely". Its only appeal were facts and truth.

Conclusion:

1) Indentations are used to help understand the epistle.
2) Christ's priesthood is not found outside of Hebrews.
3) The author used all of Scripture to validate the priesthood of Christ.
4) The profession of the Partakers is tied to Christ as high priest.
5) The profession of the Partakers is tied to Christ as The Prophet.

CHAPTER 4

"But Now We See Not"

QuickTake:

> In Hebrews Chapter 1 Christ is exalted with such terms as "heir", "excellent name", "son" and "God". In Hebrews Chapter 2 we are told that "all things [are] in subjection under his feet." But God's plan did not immediately result in kingdom glory. Rather, Hebrews 2 concludes with Jesus, not as king, but as high priest. The "Now" in the title above was a challenging time for Israelites journeying toward the Rest of God.

The resurrection of Christ was, among other things, a public demonstration of His rightful title as Son of God (Rom 1:4). Heb 1:2 describes Christ as "heir of all things, by whom also he made the worlds". And while the servant Jesus had been restored to His divine position in heaven, indications of dire, unfinished business here on earth are found in Chapter 1. Note the following:

"Hath in these last days spoken unto us by his Son..." Heb 1:2

"They shall perish...all shall wax old..." Heb 1:11

"And as a vesture shalt thou fold them up..." Heb 1:12

"...Sit on my right hand, until I make thine enemies thy footstool?" Heb 1:13

That indicated "troublous times" were ahead. They would need divine help in such times to stay on course; to run the race – to finally come to the Rest of God. Knowing Christ as The Prophet and as God's high priest was necessary for the Partakers to finish the race. Through The Prophet, they would "hear his voice", keeping them on track. Through the high priest, they would come unto God in order to "make reconciliation for the sins of the people."; thus maintaining fellowship.

So, while the emphasis in Chapter 1 was the superiority of the Son to angels, starting in Heb 1:13, the text transitions to man – the "heirs of salvation". Heb 1:13 to Heb 2:5 form a scriptural unit. The opening word of Heb 2:1 – "Therefore" – marks a continuation of the previous two verses. And, as "heirs of salvation" Heb 2:5 suggested they carried a hefty responsibility.

"Heirs of Salvation"

Whereas Heb 1:14 identified who the "heirs of salvation" were, Heb 2:5 identified who they were not. Between these verses, Heb 2:1-4 details the actions to be taken. The format below brings this to light.

> "Are they not all ministering spirits [referring to angels], sent forth to minister for them who shall be heirs of salvation?" Heb 1:14

> **[Heb 2:1-4]**

> "For unto the angels hath he not put in subjection the world to come, whereof we speak." Heb 2:5

Heb 2:5 infers the "heirs of salvation" shall have offices of authority in Christ's future kingdom. These offices were not promised to the angels. Christ spoke about this during His 3+ year earthly ministry. Note the following, all "spoken by the Lord":

> "…make him ruler over all his goods." Matt 24:47

> "…make thee ruler over many things…" Matt 25:21, 23

> "…make ruler over his household…" Luke 12:42

> "…have thou authority over ten cities." Luke 19:17

> "…Be thou also over five cities." Luke 19:19

But contrast these verses with Heb 2:8.

> "Thou hast put all things in subjection under his feet. For in that he put all in subjection under him, he left nothing that is not put under him. But now we see not yet all things put under him." Heb 2:8

Having heard all the honors and titles conferred on the risen Son of God, it is likely scoffers and wavering brethren asked the Hebrews author: "Well, if Christ has been elevated to the highest position, how come I'm not ruling over 10 cities? If all things have been put under him, why all this evil and lawlessness?"

"Merciful and Faithful High Priest"

To address doubts, it was necessary for the author to explain Christ's death. After all, who had ever heard of God dying? In addition, why would the "heir of all things" – the Son of God assume the office of high priest? The high priest of the day was a mortal man. This may have suggested to some that Christ was something less than God. These nagging doubts had to be addressed.

Heb 2:17 states:

> "Wherefore in all things it behooved him to be made like unto his brethren, that he might be a merciful and faithful high priest in things pertaining to God, to make reconciliation for the sins of the people." Heb 2:17

The Partakers most likely knew that Jesus Christ was God's high priest. However, this verse is the 1st occurrence in the Bible where that fact is in writing.

What did the high priest do?

Ellicott reminds us.

> *The characteristic function of the high priest was his presentation of the sacrifice on the Day of Atonement, that <u>expiation</u> might be made for the sins of the whole people, that the displeasure of God might not rest on the nation on account of sin.*
> *Ellicott's Commentary for English Readers*

Clearly, meeting with God had been "off limits" and extremely restricted. It occurred just one time a year and only by one man.

But Christ changed all that for the better!

Let's jump ahead to understand the positive change:

> "Wherefore he is able also to save them to the uttermost that come unto God by him, seeing he ever liveth to make intercession for them." Heb 7:25

> "Having therefore, brethren, boldness to enter into the holiest by the blood of Jesus," Heb 10:19

> "Let us draw near with a true heart..." Heb 10:22a

The vail had been torn. God was now accessible. So, how does Heb 2:17 fit in? The Partakers would no longer go to the Levitical priest to deal with their sins. Why? Because the Partakers now knew it was nothing more than a shadow system. The substance – Christ Himself – invited them to "come unto God by him". The Partakers had no need of a mortal mediator, for they had God the Son, at the right hand of God, acting as High Priest on their behalf. With "boldness", they could "enter into the holiest" and "come unto God by him, seeing he ever liveth to make intercession for them." Heb 7:25. Maintaining fellowship with God would be crucial as the Partakers ran the race.

Having done its job, the Levitical system with it Aaronic priesthood would eventually fall from its prominence. Heb 8:13 states:

> "In speaking of a new covenant, he makes the first one obsolete. And what is becoming obsolete and growing old is ready to vanish away." Heb 8:13 (ESV)

Not a Priest on Earth

But Heb 8:4 is clear that Christ's priesthood was not located on earth, but in heaven.

> "For if he were on earth, he should not be a priest, seeing that there are priests that offer gifts according to the law:" Heb 8:4

The author's approach of convincing his wavering brethren to run the race was to demonstrate the superiority of Christ and His divine priesthood to that of man and his mortal priesthood. But, since Christ had "passed into the heavens", it would be a matter of faith – "not by sight". Christ was not physically accessible; whereas the Levitical priest was. The Partakers could easily experience the Levitical law with all his senses - the temple, the sacrifices, the priests. He could see, touch, hear and smell all things associated with the shadow system. That has a strong pull to the natural man.

To counter this sensual appeal, the author devoted the bulk of Hebrews 5 through Hebrews 10 contrasting the subordinate Levitical system to the "better" priesthood of the Son of God. The intent was for The Partakers to conclude there was only one choice. They had to become fully convinced that the Levitical system could never make them "heirs of salvation" - could not take away sins. Only Christ's priesthood could do that.

From Exalted Lord to High Priest

The tone of Hebrews changes in Heb 2:8b

> "...But now we see not yet all things put under him." Heb 2:8b

Prior to this, the epistle was about the unique inheritance and "excellent name" of the risen Lord. However, starting in Heb 2:9 the subject was His oneness with the seed of Abraham and His death on their behalf. Chapter 2 concludes with Christ presented, not as the "only Potentate, king of kings and lord of lords", but as high priest. Of this office, Heb 5:4 states:

> "And no man taketh this honour unto himself, but he that is called of God, as was Aaron." Heb 5:4

The office of the high priest was appointed unto Christ "as was Aaron". Contrast this with Heb 1:8

> "But unto the Son he saith, Thy throne, O God, is for ever and ever..." Heb 1:8

It seems odd that Christ, who in the 1st chapter is presented as God, with a "more excellent name" and described as "heir of all things", was consigned to an office that mortal men had previously occupied. Why?

The answer is found at the end of Heb 2:17

> "...to make reconciliation for the sins of the people." Heb 2:17b

Making reconciliation for sins was part of the unfinished business cited at the beginning of this chapter. The Partakers had not yet entered "into his rest". They were in a race journeying toward that goal. In order to finish the race, they were exhorted in Heb 12:1 to

> "...lay aside every weight, and the sin which doth so easily beset us..."

In the past, when the Israelite sinned, he brought an animal sacrifice, whose blood appeased God for his sin. But that blood was only a type. It was a teaching tool, which had no redemptive value at all. It was part of the shadow system. But now, the Partakers had been "illuminated" and now knew the sacrificial components of the shadow system pointed to

"...the blood of Christ, who through the eternal Spirit offered himself without spot to God..." Heb 9:14

The Blood of an Animal? Or that of Christ?

Unlike members of the Body of Christ, the sins of the Partakers still needed to be dealt with in order to approach a righteous God. The major difference being that members of the Body of Christ were a new creation. They had died with Christ and to the law. They had been declared righteous. Therefore, sin is not imputed unto the members of the Body of Christ. They are under Grace, having died to the Law. (Rom 4:6-8; 5:13; 6:14).

Unlike members of the Body of Christ, the Partakers had not died with Christ or to the law upon believing. And thus, they had **not yet been declared righteous**. Therefore, making reconciliation for their sins was an on-going necessity. This contrast is explained in greater detail on page one hundred four.

Having sinned, the Partaker had a choice. What course would he take? Would he bring an animal's blood in accordance with the familiar Levitical system? Or would he put his trust on Christ's "own blood *[by which]* he entered in once into the holy place" (Heb 9:12)?

In the Old Testament, the blood of the animal made an atonement for the repentant sinner. The English word atonement is translated from a Hebrew word meaning cover (Strongs# 3722). And that's all it did: cover. Throughout his life the repentant sinner would repeat this offering over and over again. The discerning sinner would eventually figure out that the blood of the animal was not a solution. The Law could not result in perfection.

This very thing – perfection – set Christ's priesthood apart from the Levitical system. The repentant sinner needed real cleansing; not a cover. The kind that only the once-shed blood of Christ could provide.

> "How much more shall the blood of Christ, who through the eternal Spirit offered himself without spot to God, purge your conscience from dead works to serve the living God?" Heb 9:14

That Christ is the high priest ready "to make reconciliation for the sins of the people" invites the repentant sinner to come

> "...boldly unto the throne of grace, that we may obtain mercy, and find grace to help in time of need." Heb 4:16

We believe the same exhortation is found in 1John 1:7-9

> "But if we walk in the light, as he is in the light, we have fellowship one with another, and the blood of Jesus Christ his Son cleanseth us from all sin.
>
> If we say that we have no sin, we deceive ourselves, and the truth is not in us.
>
> If we confess our sins, he is faithful and just to forgive us our sins, and to cleanse us from all unrighteousness." 1John 1:7-9

John, like the author of Hebrews, is exhorting his readers to come to Christ to receive "reconciliation for...sins".

The words *purge* in Heb 9:14, *cleanseth* in 1John 1:7 and *cleanse* in 1John 1:9 are taken from the same Greek word: katharizo – Strongs# 2511.

Not a King, But a Priest

To finish the race, the Partakers needed, not a king, but a high priest to intercede to God for their sins.

By the end of Hebrews 2, the author had laid a foundation upon which the remainder of the epistle would be constructed. That foundation has two pillars: (1) Christ as The Prophet of Deut 18:15, 18 and (2) Christ as God's high priest. The Prophet is emphasized in Hebrews 3 and 4. This emphasis lies dormant for several chapters but surfaces again in Hebrews 12. Hebrews 3 and 4 took the Partakers back to "your fathers" - to "the provocation, in the day of temptation in the wilderness" (Heb 3:8). The key exhortation there being "hear his voice". More specifically, hear the voice of The Prophet. We will explore this in the next chapter.

Hebrews 5 through 10 emphasizes the office of the high priest. Whereas The Prophet is found in other parts of Scripture (Deut 18, John 1 and Acts 3), Christ as high priest is not. Therefore, the Hebrews author devoted a large segment of the letter going into the details of the priesthood. These details formed the basis for contrasting our Lord's priesthood to that of Aaron. But keep in mind, the Levitical priesthood was not some false teaching. It was a legitimate system instituted by God.* We say that to make sure one understands the contrast is not between good and evil but rather between inferior and superior; between example and the real deal.

The purpose of spelling out the priesthood in such detail was to educate and inform the wavering brethren. The revelation of Christ's priesthood as substance was to encourage the Partakers to cling to Christ Jesus, who was their One and only high priest. Ultimately, they would have to own the fact that Jesus – and Jesus alone – was "the author and finisher of our faith".

Acts 4:12 states it well

> "Neither is there salvation in any other: for there is none other name under heaven given among men, whereby we must be saved." Acts 4:12

Only after having entered into God's Rest, would they fellowship with the king.

"enter into my rest"

Where is the Rest of God? We get little information from the New Testament because Rest is, with the exception of one verse in Acts, only found in Hebrews 3 and 4. However, Psalm 95 provides a direct link from the New Testament to the Old Testament. Furthermore, upon examination of the Old Testament, a connection between Rest and Zion/Jerusalem becomes apparent.

The details of this examination is presented in the Appendix - The Rest of God. Our conclusion from this examination is that Zion and Jerusalem are on earth and not in heaven. Because the context of Hebrews 3 and 4 are centered upon "your fathers" and the "provocation, in the day of temptation in the wilderness", it follows that the Rest in these two chapters applies to the nation of Israel and God's prophetic promises to them.

From our examination, we concluded that the Rest is the habitation of God in Zion located in Jerusalem upon the earth.

Conclusion:

1) The angels were not the "heirs of salvation".
2) Christ as high priest was to "make reconciliation for the sins of the people".
3) Christ was not a priest while on earth.
4) To finish the race, the Partakers needed, not a king, but a high priest to intercede to God for their sins.
5) The Rest of God is upon the earth.

*After Israel is restored to the land, the duties of the Levitical priests will be consigned to a memorial assignment. See Jeremiah 33.

"But Now We See Not"

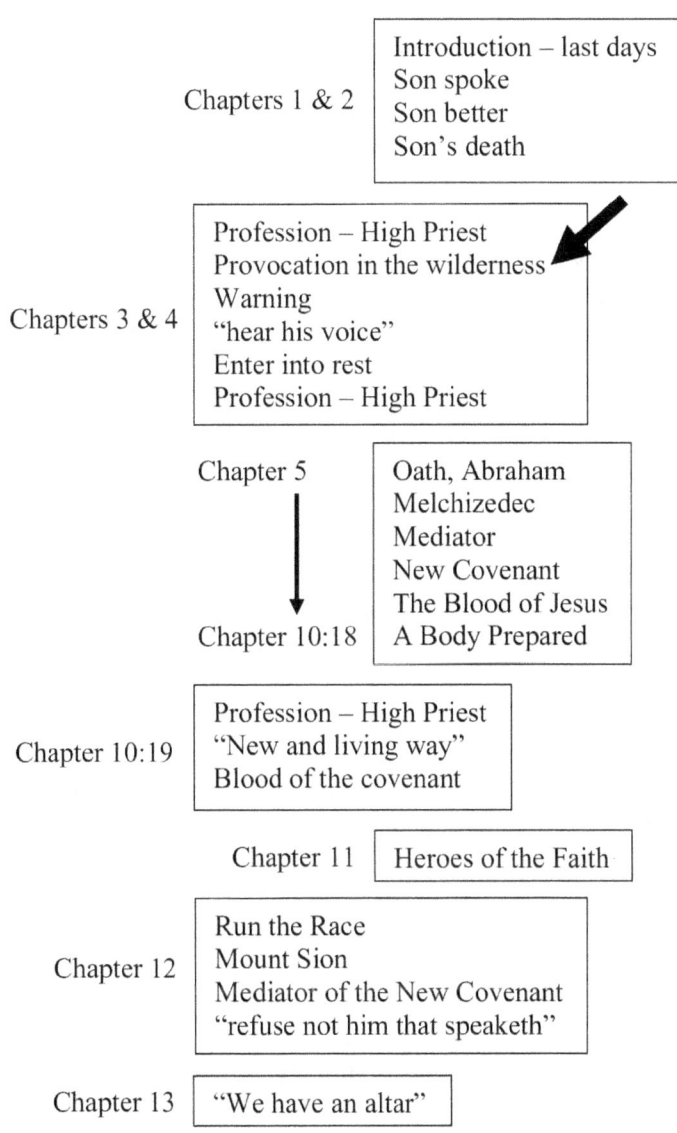

47

CHAPTER 5

"The Words Which Thou Gavest Me"

QuickTake:

> In the previous chapter we stated that the profession of Heb 3:1 and 4:14 consisted of two pillars: Christ as The Prophet and Christ as the high priest. Because The Prophet is not as recognizable as the High Priest, this chapter will explore its significance. Having a better understanding of the role of The Prophet will give us a better grasp of "our profession".

The title of this chapter is taken from John 17:8. Though not publicly declared so until Acts 3, the following verses tell us that Christ was The Prophet in the time period of Matthew, Mark, Luke and John. Christ publically credited God with the words He spoke, making sure all knew He was not the author of those words.

> "For he whom God hath sent speaketh the words of God: for God giveth not the Spirit by measure unto him." John 3:34

> "I have many things to say and to judge of you: but he that sent me is true; and I speak to the world those things which I have heard of him." John 8:26

> "He that loveth me not keepeth not my sayings: and the word which ye hear is not mine, but the Father's which sent me." John 14:24

> "Henceforth I call you not servants; for the servant knoweth not what his lord doeth: but I have called you friends; for all things that I have heard of my Father I have made known unto you." John 15:15

> "For I have given unto them the words which thou gavest me; and they have received them, and have known surely that I came out from thee, and they have believed that thou didst send me." John 17:8

"spoken by the Lord"

The 1st passage giving us understanding into the details of "our profession" is the opening verses of Hebrews 2. The passage is shown below with the secondary phrases removed.

> "Therefore we ought to give the more earnest heed to the things which we have heard…so great salvation; which at the first began to be spoken by the Lord, and was confirmed unto us by them that heard him; God also bearing them witness, both with signs and wonders, and with divers miracles, and gifts of the Holy Ghost, according to his own will?" Heb 2:1a, 3b, 4

The phrase "spoken by the Lord" included the Lord's words found in the Four Gospels and the subsequent message of Pentecost (see John 14:26). "Earnest heed" is translated "pay much closer attention" in the ESV and "pay even more attention" in the HCS. The Greek word translated "earnest" has the meaning of "exceedingly" or "beyond measure". It is Strongs# 4056.

The Hebrews 2 passage above is an amplification of the opening verses of Hebrews 1.

> "God, who at sundry times and in divers manners spake in time past unto the fathers by the prophets,
>
> Hath in these last days **spoken unto us by his Son**, whom he hath appointed heir of all things, by whom also he made the worlds;" Heb 1:1, 2

However, the exhortation in Heb 2:1 carries considerably more weight because Chapter 1 had made clear His deity and His superiority to angels.

With those two facts alone we can appreciate the intensity behind the words "earnest heed".

But its origin goes way back before the book of Hebrews to the book of Deuteronomy. The "spoken by the Lord" message of The Gospels and Pentecost goes back to Moses. Note Peter's words in Acts 3:22.

> "For Moses truly said unto the fathers, A prophet shall the Lord your God raise up unto you of your brethren, like unto me; him shall ye hear in all things whatsoever he shall say unto you." Acts 3:22

Acts 3:22 is taken from Deut 18:15-19, which was addressed to Israel alone. Gentiles were not present nor were they invited to the events in Exo 20:18, 19. That was a private meeting between God and His people Israel. Thus, the "spoken by the Lord" of Heb 2:3 are words intended for Israel and has its roots going back fifteen hundred years to Israel's exodus from Egypt (Exo 19:1-6). The words "spoken by the lord" progressed through history as follows:

Exo 20:18, 19
Deut 18:15-19
Acts 3:22
Heb 1:2
Heb 2:3

More Words

Jesus spoke the following words to His disciples on the night before the crucifixion.

> "But the Comforter, which is the Holy Ghost, whom the Father will send in my name, he shall teach you all things, and bring all

things to your remembrance, whatsoever I have said unto you." John 14:26

Note carefully, the "all things" which Christ had said to them, the Holy Spirit would teach and remind them. This is an amazing statement for Christ had said volumes (John 21:25) and mortal men would indeed need divine power to take it all in, understand it and to teach others.

What are some of the things that Christ said unto them during the time period of the Four Gospels? This question is important because the answer partially makes up the "our profession" which the Hebrews were strongly admonished to hold fast. Consider the following:

Matt 10:5, 6 → go not to the gentiles but to Israel

Matt 19:28 → the apostles judging the twelve tribes of Israel

Mark 11:10 → kingdom of David – validated in Luke 19:40

Luke 24:44 → "must be fulfilled" – Moses, prophets, Psalms

John 4:22 → salvation is of the Jews

John 12:13 → King of Israel – validated in Luke 19:40

Rom 15:8 sums up our Lord's earthly ministry.

> "Now I say that Jesus Christ was a minister of the circumcision for the truth of God, to confirm the promises made unto the fathers:" Rom 15:8

The "promises made unto the fathers" are promises made to the nation of Israel. The Lord's confirmation ministry to Israel forms part of "the things which we have heard" of Heb 2:1 – making up the "our profession" of Heb 3:1, 4:14 and 10:23.

"hear his voice"

The exhortation to give earnest heed to the words of the Son carries forward into the 3rd and 4th chapters of Hebrews. Specifically, the term is "hear his voice" found in Heb 3:7, 15 and Heb 4:7. It is a quote from Psalm 95. Jesus of Nazareth used that same phrase in John 10:3, 4:

> "...and the sheep **hear his voice**...he goeth before them, and the sheep follow him: for they know his voice" John 10:3, 4.

The key action words in John 10:3-5 are **hear** and **follow**. The picture here is a flock of sheep outside the sheepfold following the shepherd. The sheep stay on course by listening to his voice and his voice only. If a stranger calls, they will flee because they do not recognize the stranger's voice.

> "And a stranger will they not follow, but will flee from him: for they know not the voice of strangers." John 10:5

Clearly, with every step, the sheep are giving "earnest heed" to the shepherd's voice. The sheep are not relying on their sight. Similar to other animals, sheep lack a fovea (responsible for sharp central vision) which prevents them from focusing clearly on objects directly in front of them. So, they must rely on hearing in order to follow. Therefore, unable to see the shepherd in front of them, they rely on their hearing and his voice to stay on course.

One can see the analogy in Hebrews. Jesus of Nazareth has risen and is seated in heavenly places. Obviously, since He cannot be seen, the Partakers (the sheep) will have to listen attentively to the voice of the unseen shepherd in order to follow Him. The sheepfold of John 10:1-5 is a temporary dwelling. The porter is the Law. In the application to Hebrews, the shepherd is Christ as high priest leading them to their permanent dwelling – the Rest of God. He is leading them by His voice!

Unlike members of the Body of Christ (who are sealed according to Eph 1:13, 14), the Partakers had no guarantee they would arrived at the final dwelling place. To make sure their journey concluded successfully, they needed to earnestly heed the shepherd's voice all along the way. They started well but needed to finish "the race that is set before" them (Heb 12:1).

To reject The Prophet's words would be catastrophic for Acts 3:23 continues:

> "And it shall come to pass, that every soul, which **will not hear** that prophet, shall be destroyed from among the people." Acts 3:23

The "spoken by the lord" progression is updated as follows:

Exo 20:18, 19
Deut 18:15-19
Acts 3:22
Heb 1:2
Heb 2:3
Heb 3:7, 15; 4:7

"I will raise them up a Prophet"

Let's review some relevant history. Starting at Exo 20:18, 19 the Scriptures come full circle in Hebrews 12. The author of Hebrews takes the Partakers back to the mount in Horeb in order to compare the shadows with the substance. In Exo 20:18 Moses had assembled the nation Israel before the mount to hear God speak. But the people of Israel "removed" themselves and "stood afar off". They would listen to Moses – but they did not want to listen to God.

> "And all the people saw the thunderings, and the lightnings, and the noise of the trumpet, and the mountain smoking: and when the people saw it, they removed, and stood afar off.
>
> And they said unto Moses, speak thou with us, and we will hear: but let not God speak with us, lest we die." Exo 20:18, 19

Their refusal to hear God was the basis for the giving of The Prophet. It would benefit the reader to review the passage of Deut 18:15-19. Verses 16 and 17 are especially revealing for they inform us that God was keenly aware of their refusal to hear His voice.

> "According to all that thou desiredst of the LORD thy God in Horeb in the day of the assembly, saying, let me not hear again the voice of the LORD my God, neither let me see this great fire any more, that I die not.
>
> And the LORD said unto me, they have well-spoken that which they have spoken." Deut 18:16, 17

The Partakers of Hebrews were faced with a similar situation. Whereas the nation of Israel at Horeb refused to hear God's voice, the Partakers were warned "see that ye refuse not him that speaketh...from heaven".

> "For ye are not come unto the mount that might be touched, and that burned with fire, nor unto blackness, and darkness, and tempest," Heb 12:18
>
> "But ye are come unto mount Sion, and unto the city of the living God, the heavenly Jerusalem, and to an innumerable company of angels," Heb 12:22
>
> "See that ye refuse not him that speaketh. For if they escaped not who refused him that spake on earth, much more shall not we escape, if we turn away from him that speaketh from heaven:" Heb 12:25

In Hebrews 12, the author is bringing closure to God's declaration in Deut 18:19.

> "And it shall come to pass, that whosoever will not hearken unto my words which he shall speak in my name, I will require it of him." Deut 18:19

No greater warning can be given. God is going to make good on His word. Those who refuse the Son who "speaketh from heaven" will be "destroyed from among the people". There would be no second chance.

The author brought the warning home in Heb 4:7-11 concluding his thoughts with Heb 4:11

> "Let us labour therefore to enter into that rest, lest any man fall after the same example of unbelief." Heb 4:11

The "same example of unbelief" is referring to their ancestor's rejection of the Lord's voice in Horeb.

The "spoken by the lord" progression takes its final form:

Exo 20:18, 19
Deut 18:15-19
Acts 3:22
Heb 1:2
Heb 2:3
Heb 3:7, 15; 4:7
Heb 12:25

A brief summary of "our profession"

That "spoken by the Lord" in Heb 2:3 defines "our profession" as:
1) Christ's words to his disciples during the Four Gospels.
2) Christ's words "...all that the prophets have spoken: Ought not Christ to have suffered these things, and to enter into his glory?" (Luke 24:25, 26)
3) Christ's words that "all things" written by Moses, the prophets, and in the psalms must be fulfilled. (Luke 24:44).

As Hebrews declares "enter*[ing]* into his glory" would include His priesthood and His office as mediator of the New Covenant. Though the prophets may not have fully understood, they still wrote about it and, thus their writings are part of the "all things" of Luke 24:44. (1Pet 1:10, 11).

The reader is encouraged to read these passages. He will see how they link together to form God's prophetic program fulfilling the promises to the nation of Israel.

Conclusion:

1) Christ, the Son of God, is The Prophet.
2) The phrase "spoken by the Lord" demanded the utmost obedience.
3) The phrase "spoken by the Lord" included the Lord's words found in the Four Gospels and the subsequent messages of early Acts.
4) "Hear his voice" has its source in Deut 18:18, 19.
5) The events of Deut 18:16, 17 go back to Exo 20:19.
6) Per Acts 3:22, 23, the nation Israel knew full well Christ was The Prophet.
7) "our profession" is composed of "all things" Christ said to His disciples (John 14:26).
8) Christ's words to His disciples included the need to fulfill that written in Moses, the prophets and the Psalms (Luke 24:44).

"The Words Which Thou Gavest Me"

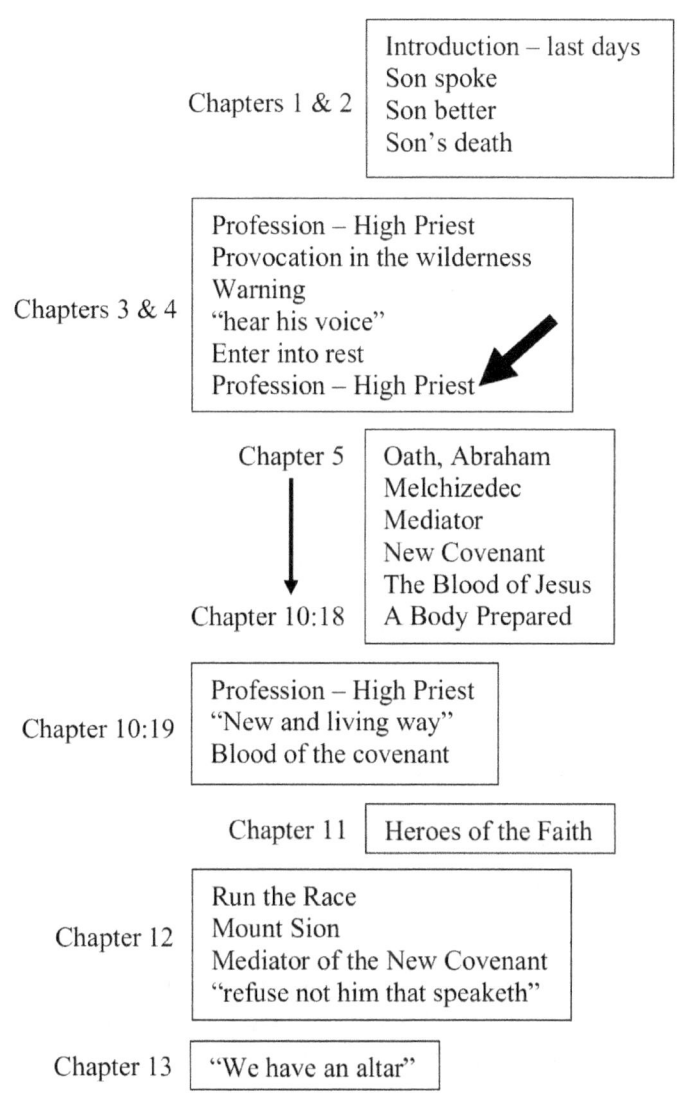

CHAPTER 6

Melchisedec

QuickTake:

> Having proclaimed Christ as high priest, the author proceeded to demonstrate the legitimacy of this high office. Since Moses spoke only of the Aaronic line, a priest outside of the tribe of Levi was not contemplated. After centuries of dormancy, the Holy Spirit awakens us to Melchisedec, the first priest found in the Scriptures.

Refer to the outline in the previous page. We are transitioning to the right side of the outline. Recall, this was not about the Partakers directly. It was important doctrinal information they needed to know in order to continue "the race that is set before us". Starting in Hebrews 5, the author embarked on a long treatise to validate the priesthood of Jesus Christ. Because there was nothing about it in the Old Testament and wanting to be thorough, it spanned several chapters. We will signal the reader when transitioning back to the left side.

Christ did not appoint Himself a high priest. He was called of God. The office of high priest does not emphasize His deity. Rather, it emphasizes His link with man and His willingness to help "his brethren". The beginning of Hebrews 5 tells us that the high priest is "taken from among men...for men". That Jesus endured the sufferings of humanity demonstrated His "all-in" genuine compassion and ability in that "he himself also *[was]* compassed with infirmity".

However, Christ's appointment to the office occurred sometime after His resurrection from the dead. Heb 5:5 tells us

> "So also Christ glorified not himself to be made an high priest; but he that said unto him, Thou art my Son, to day have I begotten thee." Heb 5:5

This quote, from Psa 2:7, speaks of the resurrection of Christ as confirmed in Acts 13:33.

> "God hath fulfilled the same unto us their children, in that he hath raised up Jesus again; as it is also written in the second psalm, Thou art my Son, this day have I begotten thee." Acts 13:33

Thus, in harmony with Heb 8:4, Christ was not a priest while on earth prior to the cross. Therefore, He could not, as some believe, have presided as a priest when He gave Himself an offering and sacrifice to God.

God's Oath

In establishing the legitimacy of Christ's priesthood after the order of Melchisedec, the author reminded the Partakers of their father Abraham. The text brings forth two points about the patriarch: (1) God's promises to him were done so by an oath and (2) Abraham was blessed by Melchisedec.

God's oath is powerful. It equates to an assurance from God. Promises founded upon God's oath will be fulfilled. God's character demands it. Though the timing may not be known, the fulfillment is assured. This is the jist of Heb 6:17, 18.

> "Wherein God, willing more abundantly to shew unto the heirs of promise the immutability of his counsel, confirmed it by an oath:
>
> That by two immutable things, in which it was impossible for God to lie, we might have a strong consolation, who have fled for refuge to lay hold upon the hope set before us:" Heb 6:17, 18

The hope is Christ Jesus (Heb 7:19; 10:22, 23). The focus of the passage above was "to lay hold upon the hope set before us". Knowing God's oath was based on "two immutable things" they could now "lay hold" with assurance and confidence.

The author used God's fulfillment of the Abrahamic promises to remind the Partakers of the significance of the oath of God. And having done so, the author applied that same oath-important significance in relating Christ's priesthood to that of Melchisedec. In short, "those priests" were not confirmed by an oath, but Christ most certainly was – and that was the difference.

"Melchizedec, king of Salem"

The first occurrence of Melchisedec occurs in Gen 14:18

> "And Melchizedek king of Salem brought forth bread and wine: and he was the priest of the most high God." Gen 14:18

Outside of Hebrews, little is known of him. Hebrews 7 fills in some additional details:

1) Melchisedec was a king (v.1)
2) Melchisedec blessed Abraham (v.1)
3) Abraham paid tithes to Melchisedec (v.2)
4) Melchisedec "abideth a priest continually" (v.3)
5) "the less [Abraham] is blessed of the better [Melchisedec]" (vv. 4 & 7)
6) Abraham is "better" than Levi (vv. 5 & 10)
7) The Levitical priest died while Melchisedec "liveth" (v.8)
8) Levi paid tithes to Melchisedec through Abraham (v.9)

Note, in the points above, how Abraham is in the "middle" between Melchisedec and the Levitical priesthood. On these points alone, one can make the conclusion that the priesthood of Melchisedec is "better" than that of Levi. These points would not be inconsequential to an Israelite. They struck at the very core of his religion – the Levitical priesthood. It was undeniable: Melchisedec was "better" than Levi. Abraham's tithing and Melchisedec's blessing confirmed it.

The author had heretofore laid down different puzzle parts. Now, in Heb 7:11, 12, he started to put them together. It began with three facts from these verses:

1) The Levitical priesthood could not deliver perfection.
2) The Levitical priesthood and the Law (referring to the 1st covenant) are closely intertwined.
3) A change in one affects the other.

That God chose another priest totally different from that of Levi, was validation of the imperfection of the 1st covenant. There were slight clues of a replacement in Scriptures; notably Psa 110:4 and Jer 31:31.

> "The LORD hath sworn, and will not repent, Thou art a priest for ever after the order of Melchizedek." Psa 110:4

> "Behold, the days come, saith the LORD, that I will make a new covenant with the house of Israel, and with the house of Judah:" Jer 31:31

Regarding Jer 31:31, the author tells us in Heb 8:13 that the word "new" made the first covenant old. Psalms was written about 1000 BC, while Jeremiah was written about 600 BC.

Bottom line: God called an altogether different priest for the promised New Covenant.

"the word of the oath"

Before we get into the details of the oath, let's not lose sight of the target community of the new covenant: the nation of Israel. While there is a clear separation in the two priesthoods: one from Levi, the other from Judah, the connection to the nation of Israel remains intact. Levi and Judah formed two of the 12 tribes of Israel. Jer 31:31 reminds us that the new covenant is "...with the house of Israel, and with the house of Judah". In summary, while the priesthood changed, the target community did not – it was to Israel.

Now note the contrast in the opening words of Heb 7:21

> "(For those priests were made **without an oath**; but this *[the Lord]* **with an oath** by him [God]..." Heb 7:21

Clearly, detached from the oath of God, the inferiority of the Aaronic priesthood was on full display. The major differences are easy to understand when one sees that one priesthood is before resurrection and the other is after. One was subject to death and corruption, while the other has an "endless life". One was subject to infirmity, while the other enjoys His rest sitting at "the right hand of the Majesty on high".

The resurrected Jesus "continueth ever" and therefore "hath an unchangeable priesthood" (Heb 7:25). This is so because it was by God's oath. And because He is an "unchangeable" priest, He is a "surety of a better" covenant. Surety is translated "the guarantee" or "the guarantor" in other translations.

In that Christ was appointed a priest after His resurrection, the author equated the "better hope" with perfection, which was something the Levitical system could not provide. Note Heb 7:19

> "For the law made nothing perfect, but the bringing in of a better hope did; by the which we draw nigh unto God." Heb 7:19

This reminds us of our Lord's words in Matt 5:48

> "Be ye therefore perfect, even as your Father which is in heaven is perfect." Matt 5:48

The author emphasized the significance of God's oath in the latter verses of Hebrews 7.

"And inasmuch as not without an oath he was made priest:" Heb 7:20

"(For those priests were made without an oath; but this with an oath by him that said unto him, The Lord sware and will not repent, Thou art a priest for ever after the order of Melchisedec:)" Heb 7:21

"For the law maketh men high priests which have infirmity; but the word of the oath, which was since the law, maketh the Son, who is consecrated [perfect] for evermore." Heb 7:28

A Recap of Hebrews 6 and 7

The author used the well-revered Abraham for two reasons:

First, all were aware that God had sworn and fulfilled promises made to Abraham. The meaning being that an oath from God equates to an assurance from God. The author carried that assurance to the priesthood of Christ in Hebrews 7, reminding his readers that the Levitical priests received no such oath. That a new priesthood was necessary, meant that the old system was not capable of providing perfection.

Second, Abraham is pictured as being in the "middle" between Melchisedec and Levi. The point was made that Melchisedec was "greater" than Abraham in that Melchisedec blessed Abraham and received tithes from the patriarch. By lineage, Abraham was "greater" than Levi (his great grandson). Therefore, Levi had a subordinate role regarding Melchisedec because Levi was "yet in the loins of his father [Abraham], when Melchisedec met him." (Heb 7:10).

Hebrews 6 and 7 are the most enlightening chapters in the epistle in that the enormity of an oath from God and the person of Melchisedec were scarcely emphasized in the Old Testament. A logical flow of the major points is given below.

1) Melchisedec is better than Abraham.
2) Abraham is better than Levi.
3) Therefore, Melchisedec is better than Levi.
4) Priesthood and covenant are closely intertwined.
5) A change in one affects the other.
6) Psa 110:4 speaks of a "for evermore" priest: Melchisedec.
7) Perfection was not by the Levitical priesthood.
8) Levitical priests gave way to an oath-confirmed "for evermore" priest.
9) Because of points 4 & 5, the first covenant will be set aside.
10) The promise of the New Covenant (Jer 31:31) will be fulfilled.
11) God will insure perfection by an oath-confirmed "for evermore" priest.

"this is the sum"

In Hebrews 8 the author did indeed "turn the page". After Hebrews 7, the following key words are not found going forward: oath, Abraham and Melchisedec. Refer to the arrow in the outline at the end of the chapter. These fundamental words, found only in Hebrews 6 and 7, were instrumental in establishing the legitimacy of the priesthood of Jesus Christ. But having made his case, the author was moving on to the duties of the priest: service in the tabernacle and the better covenant.

The sum of Hebrews 8 contains four components:

1) A high priest, not on earth, but at the right hand of God. (v.1)
2) The true tabernacle, not on earth, but heavenly and of God. (v.2)
3) A "more excellent ministry" (v.6)
4) Christ – the mediator of a better covenant. (v.6)

God's oath to Christ is the foundation upon which these four components rest.

New Words

Two words which occurred before Hebrews 6 and continued into the latter chapters of Hebrews are **high priest** and **promise**. And before concluding Hebrews 7, the author introduced a new word: **covenant**

(Strongs# 1242). In Hebrews 8, three new words are introduced: **sanctuary** (Strongs# 39), **tabernacle** (Strongs# 4633) and **mediator** (Strongs# 3316).

In Hebrews 9 the **blood** of Christ is introduced. The remainder of the Hebrew letter revolves around these key words: high priest, promise, covenant, sanctuary, tabernacle, mediator, and blood.

Conclusion:

1) God's promises to Abraham were by oath.
2) Melchisedec received tithes from Abraham and blessed him.
3) Levi paid tithes to Melchisedec through Abraham.
4) The Levitical priests were **not** appointed to their office by an oath.
5) The Levitical system could not bring perfection.
6) Perfection was by a God-appointed priest with an "endless life"
7) An "endless life" refers to the resurrection of Christ.
8) God appointed Christ high priest by an oath.
9) Like Melchisedec, Christ is both king and priest.
10) Christ's priesthood through the New Covenant will bring perfection.

Melchisedec

Chapters 1 & 2
- Introduction – last days
- Son spoke
- Son better
- Son's death

Chapters 3 & 4
- Profession – High Priest
- Provocation in the wilderness
- Warning
- "hear his voice"
- Enter into rest
- Profession – High Priest

Chapter 5
↓
Chapter 10:18
- Oath, Abraham
- Melchizedec
- Mediator
- New Covenant
- The Blood of Jesus
- A Body Prepared

Chapter 10:19
- Profession – High Priest
- "New and living way"
- Blood of the covenant

Chapter 11
- Heroes of the Faith

Chapter 12
- Run the Race
- Mount Sion
- Mediator of the New Covenant
- "refuse not him that speaketh"

Chapter 13
- "We have an altar"

CHAPTER 7

Their God - My People

QuickTake:

> Two new words were introduced near the end of Chapter 7: covenant and mediator. One of God's key blessings to the nation of Israel was the New Covenant. That the New Covenant would have a mediator and high priest apart from the tribe of Levi was a revelation found only in Hebrews.

Having introduced two new words, Heb 8:6 proclaims Christ the mediator of a covenant.

> "But now hath he obtained a more excellent ministry, by how much also he is the mediator of a better covenant, which was established upon better promises." Heb 8:6

And if one were to ask "what covenant?", the remainder of Hebrews 8 leaves no doubt. The "better covenant" of Heb 8:6 is the New Covenant of Jer 31:31.

Heb 8:8 through 12 corresponds to Jer 31:31 through 34. The reader is encouraged to read Jeremiah chapters 30 through 33.

God's Prophetic Plan for Israel

As previously stated, the New Covenant is with the nation of Israel. It is not to be confused with the "new testament" found in 2Cor 3:6. The Body of Christ is not the subject of Hebrews. God's prophetic promises found in the writings of the prophets pertain specifically to the return of a rebellious and disobedient Israel. God's "mystery among the gentiles" pertains to the Body of Christ, of which the prophets knew nothing. Col 1:26 tells us that

> "...the mystery...hath been hid from ages and from generations, but **now** is made manifest to his saints:" Col 1:26

The "ages and generations" of Col 1:26 included God's prophets to the nation of Israel.

Contrary to some who think the Body of Christ started at Pentecost, it was then that God's prophetic ministry to Israel actually went into high gear. It was at Pentecost that the Holy Spirit clearly revealed to the nation of Israel four critical titles pertaining to Jesus of Nazareth: King, Lord, Christ and The Prophet.

> "Therefore being a prophet *[David]*, and knowing that God had sworn with an oath to him, that of the fruit of his loins, according to the flesh, he would raise up Christ to sit on his throne;" Acts 2:30

> "Therefore let all the house of Israel know assuredly, that God hath made that same Jesus, whom ye have crucified, both Lord and Christ." Acts 2:36

> "For Moses truly said unto the fathers, a prophet shall the Lord your God raise up unto you of your brethren, like unto me; him shall ye hear in all things whatsoever he shall say unto you." Acts 3:22

Recall that for some period of time within His 3+ years ministry, He told his disciples to conceal His identity as Christ.

> "Then charged he his disciples that they should tell no man that he was Jesus the Christ." Matt 16:20

This was consistent with Christ speaking to the masses in parables. His disciples even questioned Him about it.

> "And the disciples came, and said unto him, Why speakest thou unto them in parables?" Matt 13:10

In the Four Gospels, there was truth, but it was shrouded in parables and lack of understanding. Some information was revealed but the full understanding was withheld. See, for example, Matt 16:21, 22; Mark 9:31, 32; Luke 9:44, 45 and Luke 18:31-34. As I told a brother recently, just because one hears the words does not mean they understand the meaning of the words.

The Prophetic Program Revealed

But at Pentecost all that changed. All became clear as a bell! Peter's message was straightforward and clear - no parables - and the identity of the One they crucified had been fully revealed. They knew assuredly. Peter did not mix words in the early chapters of Acts. He did not try to be "diplomatic" or "find a nice way" to say it. Peter charged them with the murder of their Messiah – the murder of the God-man.

Was Israel set aside at or before Pentecost? No, for God the Holy Spirit was just beginning to work with Israel. Note Peter's words to the Jewish leadership in Acts 5.

> "Then Peter and the other apostles answered and said, We ought to obey God rather than men.
>
> The God of our fathers raised up Jesus, whom ye slew and hanged on a tree.
>
> Him hath God exalted with his right hand to be a Prince and a Saviour, for to **give repentance to Israel, and forgiveness of sins.**" Acts 5:29-31

If there were ever a reason to repent, this was it. They had murdered their messiah and king. But even with innocent blood dripping from their hands, God was still willing to give them the opportunity to repent of their horrific deed and bless them with the Holy Spirit. But they had to admit it, repent of it, trust and be baptized in His name (Acts 2:38).

One last note before we move on. Recall the strong exhortation in Heb 2:1 "to give the more earnest heed to the things which we have heard…". The "things which we have heard" are identified in Heb 2:3 as that

> "…which at the first began to be spoken by the Lord, and was confirmed unto us by them that heard him;" Heb 2:3

As stated in Chapter 5, the phrase "spoken by the Lord" included the Lord's words found in the Four Gospels and the subsequent message of Pentecost. Again, read John 14:26.

Therefore, we conclude that "spoken by the Lord" along with Acts 5:31 solidly links Pentecost and the book of Hebrews to God's prophetic plan for the nation of Israel per His promises to the fathers. Acts 3:24 is very convincing.

> "Yea, and **all the prophets** from Samuel and those that follow after, as many as have spoken, have likewise foretold OF THESE DAYS." Acts3:24

Rom 15:8 reveals the contents of that "spoken by the Lord".

> "Now I say that Jesus Christ was a minister of the circumcision for the truth of God, to **confirm the promises made unto the fathers**:" Rom 15:8

Not From Levi

The text in Jeremiah 31 left out one important point. It said nothing about a change in the priesthood. It would have been perfectly normal to assume that the Levitical priest would mediate God's new covenant with Israel. But, as the book of Hebrews revealed, God had other plans to be disclosed in due time.

The Old Covenant had limitations chiefly because its method of remitting sins was based on the shed blood of an animal. Hebrews 10 reminds us:

"But in those sacrifices there is a remembrance again made of sins every year.

For it is not possible that the blood of bulls and of goats should take away sins." Heb 10:3, 4

And since the blood of animals could not "take away sins", their sins and their guilt remained. Like clockwork, these animal sacrifices were never ending (by design) and served as a reminder that their sin was ever present.

In addition, the Old Covenant had for its mediator a mortal man, who himself needed a mediator! There was nothing inherent or intrinsic about Moses, Aaron or Aaron's sons which qualified them to be a mediator. They were simply types.

But though they were types and the law made nothing perfect, the law had a purpose. The Law was to instruct the Israelites. Recall Gal 3:24

"Therefore the law was our tutor to bring us to Christ, that we might be justified by faith." Gal 3:24 (NKJV)

This yearly assembly-line of animal sacrifices by mortal priests was there to get the Israelites thinking. There were far more important matters of the law than sacrifices. Recall our Lord's words to the Pharisees:

"Woe unto you, scribes and Pharisees, hypocrites! for ye pay tithe of mint and anise and cummin, and have omitted the weightier matters of the law, judgment, mercy, and faith: these ought ye to have done, and not to leave the other undone." Matt 23:23

The Prophets

The new covenant of Jer 31:31 stands in contrast to the covenant which God had made with the post-Exodus fathers in Exo 24. Referring to the old covenant, Jer 31:32 identifies it as "my covenant" which "they brake".

In the time period of Isaiah, Jeremiah and Ezekiel, Israel's rebellious "brake" was on full display resulting in God's judgment. In Isaiah's time (~725BC), Israel was conquered leaving Judah and Jerusalem to fend for themselves. In Jeremiah's time (~600BC) Daniel and Ezekiel were taken captive to Babylon. A few years later, Jerusalem was destroyed.

But, it was during those self-destructive decades that God's news of the new covenant abounded. Literally, while Jerusalem was in the process of being destroyed, God commanded an imprisoned Jeremiah to buy land! Why? This land-purchasing command found in Jeremiah 32 was a testimony of God's promise to restore the nation of Israel to the land. God was saying in effect "buy land and be confident of your ownership for, after this temporary siege is complete, it will be restored to you. You can count on it!"

In Israel's darkest hour, God was reminding them of a bright future to come per His promise. Simultaneously, while they were surrounded by a massive Gentile superpower slowly starving them to death, God was assuring them that He would make good on His oath to their fathers to exalt Israel in the promised land.

We say all this to point out that the harsh punishment imposed upon Israel during Gentile captivity did not nullify God's promises to them. Upon fulfillment of these God-will-deliver promises, Israel will be exalted and exalted in their land. Not to minimize the spiritual promises, but returning to the land would be one of the most demonstrable expression of God's promises fulfilled.

"Their God…My People"

The title of this section occurs four times in Jeremiah: Jer 24:7; 30:22; 31:33 32:38. As the broader context of these verses is examined, it is apparent that, though the present was very bleak, God's message is about the promised future blessings to the nation of Israel. The title phrase is bolded for reference in the passages below.

Jeremiah 24
    1) "I will set mine eyes upon them for good" (v.6)
    2) "I will bring them again to this land" (v.6)
    3) "I will build them" (v.6)
    4) "I will plant them" (v.6)
    5) "I will give them an heart to know me" (v.7)
    6) **"they shall be my people, and I will be their God"** (v.7)
    7) "they shall return unto me with their whole heart." (v.7)
    8) "...and they shall dwell in their own land." (v.8)

Jeremiah 30
    1) "...I will cause them to return to the land" (v.3)
    2) "... the city *[Jerusalem]* shall be builded." (v.18)
    3) "...I will multiply them..." (v.19)
    4) "...I will also glorify them..." (v.19)
    5) **"ye shall be my people, and I will be your God"** (v.22)

Jeremiah 31
    1) "I will make a new covenant with...Israel, and...Judah" (v.31)
    2) "put my law in their inward parts" (v. 33)
    3) "write it *[my law]* in their hearts" (v. 33)
    4) **"I...will be their God, and they shall be my people"** (v. 33)
    5) "they shall all know me" (v. 34)
    6) "I will forgive their iniquity" (v. 34)
    7) "I will remember their sin no more" (v. 34)
    8) "the city *[Jerusalem]* shall be built to the LORD" (v. 38)

Jeremiah 32
    1) "I will gather them out of all countries" (v.37)
    2) **"And they shall be my people, and I will be their God"** (v.38)
    3) "I will give them one heart" (v.39)
    4) "I will make an everlasting covenant with them" (v.40)
    5) "I will put my fear in their hearts" (v.40)
    6) "they shall not depart from me" (v. 40)
    7) "I will plant them in this land" (v.41)
    8) "take witnesses...about Jerusalem...cities of Judah" (v.44)
    9) "I will cause their captivity to return" (v.44)

These passages tell the story of God making good on His promise to a captive nation held in bondage due to their rebellion and disobedience. The general message of these four passages is that God will gather His people, plant them in their land, give them a new heart, multiply them and declare Israel "my people" and He "their God".

Whereas in Jer 31:31, it is labeled the "new covenant", in Jer 32:40 it is labeled the everlasting covenant. We believe the similarity of the future blessings shown in the four Jeremiah passages demonstrate they are one and the same covenant. We note that the term "everlasting covenant" occurs one time in the New Testament; in the book of Hebrews.

> "Now the God of peace, that brought again from the dead our Lord Jesus, that great shepherd of the sheep, through the blood of the everlasting covenant," Heb 13:20

The inward parts, the heart, fear, forgiveness and "their God...my people" in the passages are references to spiritual blessings. But just as important was Israel's return to the promised land and the rebuilding of Jerusalem. Though physical by nature, the return and the rebuilding are still spiritual blessings from God. Other Old Testament passages tie the "everlasting covenant" with the physical blessing of the land:

> "Which covenant he made with Abraham, and his oath unto Isaac; And confirmed the same unto Jacob for a law, and to Israel for an everlasting covenant: Saying, Unto thee will I give the land of Canaan, the lot of your inheritance:" Psa 105:9-11 (See 1Chr 16:16-18.)

> "...in **their land** they shall possess the double: everlasting joy shall be unto them...I will direct their work in truth, and I will make an **everlasting covenant** with them." Isa 61:7, 8

> "And they shall **dwell in the land** that I have given unto Jacob my servant ...and my servant David shall be their prince for ever. Moreover I will make a covenant of peace with them; it shall be

an **everlasting covenant** with them: and I will place them, and multiply them..." Eze 37:25, 26

Regarding the last passage, recall that Jeremiah and Ezekiel were contemporaries.

> Since returning to the land and the rebuilding of Jerusalem is a very integral part of God's promise contained in the New Covenant, it is clear that, at the time of the writing of Hebrews, the New Covenant was still a future event.

Back to Chapter 8

A review of the sum of the opening verses of Chapter 8 is:
1) The resurrected Christ is a forever-perfect high priest in heaven.
2) The true tabernacle is in heaven.
3) Christ received a more excellent ministry.
4) Christ is a mediator of a better covenant.

Here we learn that Christ is both high priest and mediator. Furthermore, Heb 8:4 contains a fifth point, which would have practical significance to the Partakers.

> "For if he were on earth, he should not be a priest, seeing that there are priests that offer gifts according to the law:" Heb 8:4

The following edited paragraph was taken from my 2nd book: DIED WITH CHRIST; pp. 15 & 16.

Heb. 7:28 and 8:4, 5 are super instructive - Christ could not exercise His superior priesthood here on the earth! Why not? Because there was an existing priesthood already in place – the Levitical priesthood. The two priesthoods existed simultaneously, but they could not exist in the same location - earth. That tells us that even though the priesthood was "changing" and the commandment "is...disannulling", the Levitical priesthood was still authoritative and binding at the time the Hebrew letter was penned. And where did the Levitical priests get their authority to "offer" and "serve"? From the Law – for Heb. 7:28 states: "...the law maketh men high priests...".

This is a black and white matter. There are no gray areas. The discerning Partakers understood they could only follow one priesthood. The author, in Hebrews 6 and 7, had overwhelmingly proven Christ was uniquely qualified and had the better priesthood. And now, to make it more black and white, His priesthood with its "excellent ministry" was in heaven. There was NOTHING on earth whereby the "partakers of the heavenly calling" could approach God.

"Reconciliation for the sins of the people" by God's high priest meant the people had to let go of their earthly ties and "entereth into that within the veil". They would no longer participate in animal sacrifices; either locally or in Jerusalem. Having been enlightened of the immeasurable superiority of Christ's sacrifice over that of an animal, they would certainly not take part in animal sacrifices any longer. Instead of bringing blood, they would look toward heaven and "offer" the once-shed blood of Christ to the true high priest, who was sitting on the right hand of God ready to make "intercession for them".

> "Let us draw near with a true heart in full assurance of faith, having our hearts sprinkled from an evil conscience, and our bodies washed with pure water." Heb 10:22

It would take faith to follow the unseen substance.

Heaven or Earth?

Many commentators, believing Hebrews was written to the Body of Christ, take the "heavenly calling" of Heb 3:1 as validation, citing Phil 3:14 as support for their view point. They contend that "the heavenly calling" was not just from heaven but, very importantly "to heaven" itself. But Phil 3:14 does not actually declare what they claim Heb 3:1 is stating. They are reading their viewpoints into the verses.

Applying Phil 3:14 to Heb 3:1 involves an assumption – a kind of circular reasoning. Namely that since, in their minds, Paul wrote Hebrews, Heb 3:1 must align doctrinally with Phil 3:14. In the Greek, Phil 3:14 contains "the upward calling".

But if the author's intent all along was to encourage and promote a heavenly home for the Partakers, why even bring up Christ's priestly location in Heb 8:4? It would not matter to heaven-bound believers if there were Levitical priests offering gifts on the earth.

We don't find any such similar statements in Paul's epistles. We submit Heb 8:4 infers Christ's eventual return to earth. Note Peter's words in Acts 3:19-21

> "Repent ye therefore, and be converted, that your sins may be blotted out, when the times of refreshing shall come from the presence of the Lord;
>
> And he shall send Jesus Christ, which before was preached unto you:
>
> Whom the heaven must receive until the times of restitution of all things, which God hath spoken by the mouth of all his holy prophets since the world began." Acts 3:19-21

Peter's Pentecostal passage above makes up part of the message "spoken by the Lord, and was confirmed unto us by them that heard him" of Heb 2:3. We repeat, the author began Heb 2 by strongly exhorting The Partakers to "give the more earnest heed to the things which we have heard" (Heb 2:1).

Since the risen Christ was located in heaven, His call to them was "heavenly". But their long-term hope was to live safely in the promised land – to enter "into his rest" in Jerusalem/Zion – on earth.

> "And he shall send Jesus Christ, which before was preached unto you:" Acts 3:20

Conclusion:

1) As God's high priest, Christ is the mediator of the New Covenant of Jer 31:31.
2) God's New Covenant was with the nation of Israel.
3) Pentecost was an opportunity for Israel to repent; receive remission of sins - Acts 5:31.
4) The Levitical priesthood could not take away sins.
5) News of the New Covenant was revealed around the time of Jeremiah, Ezekiel and Daniel.
6) The New Covenant of Jer 31:31 is the same as the Everlasting Covenant of Jer 32:40.
7) Other scriptures equate the Everlasting Covenant with a return to the promised land.
8) Christ has never been a priest on earth.
9) Christ will return to earth.

Their God – My People

Chapters 1 & 2
- Introduction – last days
- Son spoke
- Son better
- Son's death

Chapters 3 & 4
- Profession – High Priest
- Provocation in the wilderness
- Warning
- "hear his voice"
- Enter into rest
- Profession – High Priest

Chapter 5 → **Chapter 10:18**
- Oath, Abraham
- Melchizedec
- Mediator
- New Covenant
- The Blood of Jesus
- A Body Prepared

Chapter 10:19
- Profession – High Priest
- "New and living way"
- Blood of the covenant

Chapter 11
- Heroes of the Faith

Chapter 12
- Run the Race
- Mount Sion
- Mediator of the New Covenant
- "refuse not him that speaketh"

Chapter 13
- "We have an altar"

CHAPTER 8

Blood 101

QuickTake:

> Hebrews 8 introduced us to two words: **Covenant** and **Mediator**. In Hebrews 9 another word was introduced: the **Blood** of Christ. Hebrews 9 compares the two covenants. And though the covenants are vastly different, both are enacted by blood and pertain to the nation of Israel.

Blood (Strongs# 129) is one of those key words which appears toward the end of Hebrews. Similarly, covenant (Strongs# 1242) is also found in the latter half of the book of Hebrews. Both words occur most often in Hebrews 9 than in any other chapter.

Hebrews 7 explained how Christ's priesthood was far superior to that of Levi. Hebrews 8 revealed that the resurrected Lord was God's mediator of the New Covenant found in Jeremiah 31. In Hebrews 9, the author differentiated the tabernacles: that "made by hands" with the "greater and more perfect tabernacle".

At least four times prior to Chapter 9, the author had encouraged his readers to "come boldly", "lay hold", "draw nigh" and "come unto" the throne of grace.

> "For we have…an high priest…in all points tempted like as we are, yet without sin. Let us therefore **come boldly** unto the throne of grace…" Heb 4:15, 16

> "…we might have a strong consolation…to **lay hold** upon the hope…which entereth into that within the veil…Jesus, made an high priest…" Heb 6:18-20

"...a priest for ever after the order of Melchisedec...a better hope...by the which we **draw nigh** unto God...an oath *he was made priest.*" Heb 7:17, 19, 20

"But this man...hath an unchangeable priesthood. Wherefore he is able also to save them to the uttermost that **come unto** God by him..." Heb 7:24, 25

Note, in every one of the four come-unto-God verses above, Christ is presented as the high priest. Though, Hebrews revealed Christ as the mediator of the New Covenant, the Partakers were not invited to seek Him as such. Their point of divine contact was with a high priest - sin was still an issue and had to be dealt with (Heb 2:17).

What, How & Where

Because of Christ's unchangeable priesthood, the Israelites now had opportunity to draw near to God – directly and personally. This constitutes the "WHAT" of the author's message. That the ordinary Israelite now have access to God's tabernacle was a truly radical idea! So new and foreign was this incredible truth, that the author had repeated it several times.

But in Chapter 9, the focus turned to "WHERE" and "HOW". The "WHERE" pertained to the worship service within the true tabernacle; the "HOW" pertained to blood. The common Israelite had lots of experience with the shedding of blood (the "HOW") but none regarding access to the tabernacle (the "WHERE").

Recall from Leviticus that after the Israelite presented his offering, he, not the priest, killed the animal. Only after the blood was shed, could the priest gather the blood and apply it to the altar. But for fear of death, the Israelite would only get so close to the tabernacle (Num 18:22). So while he was literally "hands on" regarding blood, the common Israelite was a fearful and distant "hands off" regarding the tabernacle.

But now, the author of Hebrews told his readers that they, indeed could come "within the veil", into the tabernacle and "draw nigh unto God". The Israelite no longer needed a mortal man between himself and God. He could "come boldly unto the throne of grace". He could come inside the tabernacle! What had happened to make it so?

Blood 101

Before we move on, it's important that we Gentiles get a solid understanding of the key component regarding worship in the Old Covenant: blood. Worship centered around the shedding of blood. Chiefly because a Holy God was meeting with sinful men.

> "For the life of the flesh is in the blood: and I have given it to you upon the altar to make an atonement for your souls: **for it is the blood that maketh an atonement for the soul**." Lev 17:11

Blood pervaded the life of the Israelites. Recall these familiar examples:

The blood was applied to the lintel and the two side posts at the Passover (Exo 12:23).
The Old Covenant was ratified with blood and sprinkled on the people (Exo 24:8).
Daily, the blood was applied to the horns of the altar (Exo 29:12).
Daily, the blood was sprinkled around the altar (Exo 29:16).
The sprinkling of the blood on the vail and altar of incense (Lev 4:5-7).
The sprinkling of the blood on the mercy seat (Lev 16:14).
The blood was applied to Aaron's ear, thumb and foot (Exo 29:20).
It was used to purify a worshipper's home (Lev 14:52).
In accordance with their ceremonial calendar, every year over 1000 animals shed their blood.

Its consequential power is revealed in Heb 9:7 with the understated phrase "not without blood"

"But into the second went the high priest alone once every year, **not without blood**, which he offered for himself, and for the errors of the people:" Heb 9:7

This is important to comprehend because Hebrews 9 shifts the reader's attention from the blood of animals to the blood of Christ. The blood of the animals was nothing more than a type. And though it resolved nothing, the act of shedding blood was very revealing and instructive. It helped the discerning Israelite understand why Christ had to die. The type pointed to and shed light on the reality.

"The Holy Spirit this signifying"

Remarkably, it wasn't until the 9th chapter of Hebrews that the epistle first spoke of the blood of Christ:

> "But Christ being come an high priest of good things to come, by a greater and more perfect tabernacle, not made with hands, that is to say, not of this building;" Heb 9:11

> "Neither by the blood of goats and calves, but by his own blood he entered in once into the holy place, having obtained eternal redemption for us." Heb 9:12

The "not" of Heb 9:11 and the "neither" of Heb 9:12 speak of the impotency of the first covenant. This inability is emphasized in Heb 9:8.

> "The Holy Ghost this signifying, that the way into the holiest of all was not yet made manifest, while as the first tabernacle was yet standing:" Heb 9:8

The "this" of the verse above is the "alone once every year" of Heb 9:7. Aaron could only meet with God once a year. And even as the years progressed, Aaron's access remained fixed. Year after year, he could only meet with God on one day – no more. It did not appear that any progress was being made. It'd be one thing if Aaron was allowed to meet with God longer or even additional days as the years went by. That would indicate some headway toward getting closer to God. But no – just one day – year after year. Under this system there was no direct access to God and, more importantly, no hope of achieving it. This is what I think the Holy Spirit was signifying in Heb 9:8.

Was it pointless? Not at all; the Law and the first covenant taught many valuable lessons. Matt 23:23 speaks of the weightier matters: truths God wanted the Israelites to learn; chiefly "judgment, mercy, and faith". Gal 3:24 states that the law was "our schoolmaster to bring us unto Christ".

The law taught by repetition. After hundreds of years and the sacrifice of thousands of animals dictated by the law, the Israelite would learn a key point: taking away sins required death – they walked hand in hand. And thus over the centuries, two key points were fused into the mind of the Israelite: (1) taking away sins required the shedding of blood and (2) the blood of animals had obvious redemptive limitations.

But after Pentecost, upon hearing of the shed blood of Christ, it would not be foreign for the worshipper to consider the redemptive attributes of Christ's blood regarding sins and transgressions. The Israelite could reasonably pivot from the animal's blood to Christ's blood as a means of taking away sin and also for ratifying a covenant.

After Pentecost, Isaiah 53 would be understood in a whole new light. The identity of the "man of sorrows" having been revealed (Acts 8:30 35), the Isaiah passage clearly sets forth, not an animal, but a man bearing the sins of others. This would certainly have encouraged the Israelite to consider the sin-resolving authority and power of the blood of Christ.

> After Pentecost, taking away sins was still by the shedding of blood. But now it had been revealed that the ONLY shed blood that mattered was that of Christ.

"But Christ"

Jamieson, Fausett and Brown indicate the phrase "But Christ" of Heb 9:11 is in contrast to and answers the "could not make…perfect" of Heb 9:9.

> "Which was a figure for the time then present, in which were offered both gifts and sacrifices, that **could not make him that did the service perfect**, as pertaining to the conscience;" Heb 9:9

> "**But Christ** being come an high priest of good things to come, by a greater and more perfect tabernacle, not made with hands, that is to say, not of this building;" Heb 9:11

While the repetitive Law sacrifices came up short, perfection would be achieved by a better hope: a "forever-priest" and the genuine redemptive blood – that of Christ. Perfection, conscience and the removal of guilt are closely related. Heb 9:11 contains three components required to realize the fulfillment of the "promise of eternal inheritance". The meaning of eternal leaning toward **permanency**.

1) Christ as high priest
2) "Good things that have come"
3) A perfect tabernacle.

The terms "being come" and "to come" of Heb 9:11 are both aorist participles. This indicates past tense, suggesting that the "good things" had already come. The "good things" were known. These included the better promises, the near-pending New Covenant, inheritance and specifically, perfection; which the first covenant could not provide.

What had been absent for centuries had finally come. What the endless, repetitive sacrifices alluded to but could not provide was imminent - perfection.

Heb 10:1 repeats the limitations of Heb 9:9.

> "For the law having a shadow of good things to come, and not the very image of the things, can never with those sacrifices which they offered year by year continually make the comers thereunto **perfect**." Heb 10:1

Now, with Christ as the true high priest, everything changed - God was now accessible. I believe this is the best part of the "good things" that had come. Indeed, not only was He approachable, God was **inviting** the common Israelite to come unto Christ as high priest "within the veil".

It's important to keep in mind that the realization of the better promises, the better covenant, inheritance and perfection, though unseen (Heb 2:8), were NOW within a short reach because of the oath God made to Christ. With the resurrection of Christ, these blessings went from centuries of "pending" to "it's about to happen".

The Blood of Christ

The extraordinary value of the blood of Christ becomes ever more apparent because Christ was not under the penalty of death. Whereas the animal had no choice, it would eventually die. But Christ offered Himself to die. The death of Christ was exceptionally unique in that ONLY it could legally and permanently answer death's legal claim over mankind.

The animal's blood was limited to the purifying of the flesh; Heb 9:13 - it did nothing about the conscience. So, how would Christ's blood result in the worshipper being "perfect, as pertaining to the conscience" (Heb 9:9) – and what does that mean? To answer this, we go back to the Old Testament and ask: How did the animal's blood purge the flesh from defilement? Regarding a typical worshipper, was his flesh different after the blood was applied to the burnt altar? No, nothing had changed.

However, the flesh was purged because the worshipper believed there was value in the animal's blood. That value was based solely on the fact that it was God Himself Who established the animal sacrifices. Though he did not understand how the animal's blood took away sins, the worshipper obeyed and trusted God, resulting in a sweet savor and an upright relationship between God and sinner.

Physically, the animal's blood did nothing. The worshipper was purged simply by God's word. But, by design, the blood of the animal had limitations: (1) it was repetitive, (2) sin was not removed from his consciousness and (3) sin still reigned. After the worshipper offered the sacrifice, he still struggled with sin. The animal's blood did not remove his predisposition toward sin. The "old man" was still alive and well. Within weeks, the worshipper would return to sacrifice another animal due to his sin.

Benson shares his thoughts:

> *"because the worshippers once purged"* — *Or fully discharged from the guilt of their transgressions; "should have had no more conscience of sin"* — *There would have remained no more sense of guilt upon their consciences to have troubled them, and no more fear of future punishment in consequence thereof. But it was not so with them, as appears by the yearly repetition of these sacrifices, wherein there was a continual* **remembrance** *made of sin* — *A consciousness of their sins, as unpardoned, still remained even after those sacrifices were offered, as is evident from this, that in the annual repetition of their sacrifices, the people's sins, for which atonement had formerly been made, were* **remembered**; *that is, confessed as needing a yet further expiation.*
> *Joseph Benson Commentary on the Old and New Testaments; Heb 10:2, 3*

However, the discerning worshipper would come to realize that animal sacrifices were temporary and had obvious limitations. Surely, there must be something more! What would the worshipper place his hope upon? If the blood of an animal did not result in perfection, what would?

Only the blood of Christ could do that.

> "How much more shall the blood of Christ, who through the eternal Spirit offered himself without spot to God, purge your conscience from dead works to serve the living God?" Heb 9:14

To "purge your conscience from dead works" meant to discard the temporary and limited shadows of the Law and embrace/trust the permanent, sin-resolving work of Christ. That meant no more sacrifices for sin "for this he did once" (Heb 7:27). Christ's blood was unique. For only it possessed actual redemptive authority and power. This is what the Partakers had to come to grips with – and, embrace it by faith.

Unlike the Old Covenant worshipper who had no idea how the animal's blood purified him, the Partakers had been illuminated and empowered by the Holy Spirit at Pentecost. They had been illuminated as to the actual "how to" of taking away sins – the offering of Christ's blood; the only blood that mattered. Christ was the substance. All before Him were types that pointed toward Him. The "there must be something more" had been revealed. But, knowledge itself does not take away sins – it must be applied by faith.

The God-man, who was not subject to death, volunteered to die for all. And in so doing, removed death's claim upon all mankind. The author had explained this in Heb 2:14. This was a tremendous revelation from God to the Partakers.

Unlike the animal's blood, Christ's blood provided "eternal redemption".

> "Neither by the blood of goats and calves, but by his own blood he entered in once into the holy place, having obtained eternal redemption for us." Heb 9:12

At Pentecost, the Holy Spirit had unmasked the identity of Jesus of Nazareth to all: King, Lord, Christ, The Prophet and Son of God. And now, by the 9th chapter of Hebrews, the Partakers could add high priest and mediator to that list.

Conclusion:

1) The common Israelite was "hands on" regarding blood. But had no contact with the tabernacle.
2) The worship life of an Israelite revolved around the shedding of blood.
3) The high priest was the only Israelite that had any contact with God.
4) The high priest entered the Holy of Holies only one time a year.
5) The common Israelite could directly approach God through the priesthood of Christ.
6) Whereas the blood of the animal was limited to the purification of the flesh, the blood of Christ could make the worshipper perfect – remove the guilt of sin.
7) But now, because of the blood of Christ, God was inviting the common Partaker to "come boldly", "lay hold", "draw nigh" and "come unto" the throne of grace.

Blood 101

| Chapters 1 & 2 | Introduction – last days
Son spoke
Son better
Son's death |

| Chapters 3 & 4 | Profession – High Priest
Provocation in the wilderness
Warning
"hear his voice"
Enter into rest
Profession – High Priest |

| Chapter 5 ↓ Chapter 10:18 | Oath, Abraham
Melchizedec
Mediator
New Covenant
The Blood of Jesus ←
A Body Prepared |

| Chapter 10:19 | Profession – High Priest
"New and living way"
Blood of the covenant |

| Chapter 11 | Heroes of the Faith |

| Chapter 12 | Run the Race
Mount Sion
Mediator of the New Covenant
"refuse not him that speaketh" |

| Chapter 13 | "We have an altar" |

CHAPTER 9

"A Better Covenant"

QuickTake:

> In the Old Testament blood was typically shed for the atonement of sins. The 1st few chapters of Leviticus instructed the Israelites on the specifics of animal sacrifices. But the shedding of blood had another purpose which was just as important: the rarely-performed ratification of a covenant.

The priesthood was the primary focus of Hebrews 7. But in Hebrews 8 and 9 the focus transitioned toward the mediator. This word occurs three times in Hebrews (Heb 8:6; 9:15; 12:24). In Heb 8:6 we first learned that Christ is the "mediator of a better covenant". And the rest of Hebrews 8 clearly tells us that the "better covenant" is the New Covenant of Jeremiah 31.

However, it is important to remember that though the blood of the New Covenant had been shed and Christ had been appointed mediator of the New Covenant, the New Covenant was and is still future. At the time of the writing of Hebrews, it had not been established on the earth. Israel had not been "plant[ed] in the land" (Jer 32:41). Jerusalem would be destroyed and be rebuilt again (Jer 30:18; 31:38; 32:44). See pages seventy three and seventy four.

The New Covenant, like the Old of Exodus 24, would require blood for ratification. Thus, beginning in Hebrews 9, God had the Hebrews author review the history of blood regarding redemption and explain its role in the not-so-familiar making of a covenant.

From Paul's writings, we are well familiar with the redemptive power of the blood of Christ which was foundational in making us "free from the law of sin and death." (Rom 8:2). These example verses provide the foundation for "Christ died for our sins".

> "...redemption...in Christ Jesus...through faith in his blood..." Rom 3:24, 25

> "...Christ died for us...justified by his blood..." Rom 5:8, 9

> "In whom we have redemption through his blood..." Eph 1:7; Col 1:14

So to help our understanding in the area of covenant-making, the Hebrews author segmented Chapter 9 into passages of contrast and comparison as follows:

1) Heb 9:1-10 contrasted with Heb 9:11-15.
2) Heb 9:16-22; demonstrating the need for blood in both covenants.
3) Heb 9:23-28 contrasting blood (v.23), location (v.24) and frequency (v.25-28).

The main point of Heb 9:11-15 is making good on the "promise of eternal inheritance" in order to "serve the living God". The contextual meaning of the word "eternal" is not infinite duration or forever-ness. Rather, the emphasis is on finality due to genuineness. The contrast is permanency verses transience.

In Heb 9:12 eternal redemption through Christ's blood is the substance while the redemption of the Passover lamb was the type.

In Heb 9:14 eternal spirit refers to the work of the Holy Spirit resulting in the real tabernacle by way of the offering of Christ. This is in contrast to Exodus 35 where the same Holy Spirit was engaged in the making of the man-made tabernacle (Exo 35:21, 31). Bezaleel, from the tribe of Judah, was a type of Christ whom the Lord "hath filled him with the spirit of God...in all manner of workmanship".

In Heb 9:15 eternal inheritance is the substance while the apportioned lots in the land of Canaan were the types.

The Same Shed Blood

Because of the unique redemptive authority and power of Christ's blood, only it could realize the transition from the Old Covenant to the New Covenant. Regarding the Old Covenant, transgressions had occurred and had to be dealt with as dictated in the Old Testament. This was not an option. Take, for example, Deut 27:26.

> "Cursed be he that confirmeth not all the words of this law to do them. And all the people shall say, Amen." Deut 27:26

Christ died to redeem the transgressors of the Old Covenant. He took on the curse. This is the significance of the middle portion of Heb 9:15

> "…by means of death, for the redemption of the transgressions that were under the first testament…" Heb 9:15

The New Covenant could not be enacted until the Old Covenant had been brought to a rightful and legal conclusion. Sins had to be dealt with. All terms of the Exodus 24:8 contract had to be executed in order to bring closure. This is very important. A new agreement could not be implemented until all terms of the previous agreement had been completely satisfied and brought to a "contractual" conclusion. Christ removing the debt due to sins incurred under the Old Covenant is the meaning of "He taketh away the first" of Heb 10:9.

> "Then said he, Lo, I come to do thy will, O God. He taketh away the first, that he may establish the second." Heb 10:9

All this to say that the same blood poured out in order to "close out" the Old Covenant was also the same blood poured out to ratify the New Covenant. It was the same blood, having a different purpose.

Ellicott shares the following on the subject.

> *So far our thought has rested on the removal of the results of the past. The covenant and the promise relate to the establishment of the better future. Death was necessary alike for both. The offering of Christ's life (Matthew 20:28) was a ransom or an offering for sin; it was also a sacrifice inaugurating a new covenant, which contained the promise of the eternal inheritance.*
> *Ellicott's Commentary for English Readers*

The church, the Body of Christ, was redeemed with covenant-ratifying blood. But that does not mean the church is directly partaking in the New Covenant of Jeremiah 31. There are distinctions on how the Lord's shed blood affected different groups.

For the Body of Christ it represents our death - His death for our death. For the Partakers, their death was never considered. For them, the Lord's death resulted in the shed blood which was to be "brought within the vail" permitting one-to-one access to God apart from a mortal mediator.

For the Body of Christ, the results of the Lord's blood were immediate (Eph 1:13).

For the Partakers, the results were mercy and grace in time of need provided they came "boldly unto the throne of grace" offering the shed blood of their Messiah. They were in a race to "enter my rest" - it was not immediate.

The next chapter contains more details on these distinctions. But distinctions do not exclude similarities. Since inheritance, eternal life, righteousness, perfection and such terms are fully applicable to both Israel and the Body of Christ, we are not surprised that The Church partakes in Israel's "spiritual things" (Rom 15:27).

Some point out that Heb 8:8-12 is completely spiritual - that it does not refer to the land, sacrifices or to a king sitting on a throne. From this they infer Hebrews has a direct application to the church, the Body of Christ. However, the strong textual similarity of the Jeremiah passages found on pages seventy three and seventy four demonstrate that Israel's return to the promised land and the restoration of Jerusalem is clearly an integral part of the New Covenant, of which the church, the Body of Christ is not included nor partakes.

Types and Realities

To make sure his readers fully understood the necessity of the death of Christ, the author cited the dedication of Israel's first covenant in Exodus 24, which Heb 9:23 reminds us were "patterns of things in the heavens".

In the Exodus passage (Exo 24:3-8) there are two types and two realities. The two types are Moses (as mediator) and the animal's blood. The two realities are the word of God and the people.

> "And he took the book of the covenant, and read in the audience of the people: and they said, All that the LORD hath said will we do, and be obedient.
>
> And Moses took the blood, and sprinkled it on the people, and said, Behold the blood of the covenant, which the LORD hath made with you concerning all these words." Exo 24:7, 8

Note the interaction of these four components: Moses, the animal's blood, the word of God and the people. The people, in the presence of Moses, heard the word of God and declared their obedience. After which, the blood of the covenant was sprinkled upon the people. Death was required for the ratification of the covenant. At this point, the covenant (think of a contract) was sealed.

Since the "patterns of things" must be followed, let's correlate the things of Exodus with the things of Hebrews. The two realities from Exodus stay the same: the people and the word of God. However, in Hebrews, the two types in Exodus give way to the realities: (1) Christ as mediator and (2) the blood of Christ.

In Exo 24, the people were in the presence of the mediator when they heard his words and declared their obedience. Thereafter, Moses sprinkled the animal's blood on the people and ratified the covenant.

What was the word of God set forth by the author of Hebrews? How could the Hebrews' readers declare their obedience in the presence of the real mediator?

The answer to the 1st question is found in Heb 2:1, 3

> "Therefore we ought to **give the more earnest heed to the things which we have heard**, lest at any time we should let them slip." Heb 2:1

> "How shall we escape, if we neglect so great salvation; which at the first began to be **spoken by the Lord**, and was confirmed unto us by them that heard him;" Heb 2:3

"earnest heed" is obedience to that "spoken by the Lord" – the word of God.

To answer the 2nd question, we must remember that Christ's "more excellent ministry" could not be found on earth according to Heb 8:4. Thus, the worshipper, rather than going to a man-made tabernacle, went to the real mediator. The true tabernacle did not exist on earth Heb 9:24 states:

> "For Christ is…entered…into **heaven itself**, now to appear in the presence of God for us:" Heb 9:24

That is the new meeting place. Thus, the worshippers were exhorted

> "…to enter **into the holiest** by the blood of Jesus," Heb 10:19

The two types and two realities on earth had given way to the four realities in heaven. The New Covenant is ratified only with those who go to Christ "through the veil". And similar to the people in Exo 24 who were sprinkled with the animal's blood by Moses, those who "draw near with a true heart" will receive "the blood of sprinkling" from Christ. Heb 12:22, 24 states:

> "But ye are come unto mount Sion, and unto the city of the living God, the **heavenly** Jerusalem...And to Jesus the mediator of the new covenant, and to the **blood of sprinkling**..." Heb 12:22, 24

All realities meet in heaven.

Perfection

> "For the law having a shadow of good things to come, and not the very image of the things, can never with those sacrifices which they offered year by year continually make the comers thereunto perfect.
>
> For then would they not have ceased to be offered? because that the worshippers once purged should have had no more conscience of sins.
>
> But in those sacrifices there is a remembrance again made of sins every year.
>
> For it is not possible that the blood of bulls and of goats should take away sins." Heb 10:1-4

Clearly, perfection is the prize identified in Heb 10:1. The meaning of the word perfect is found in the verses which follow, with Heb 10:4 summing it up. The blood of animals, even if flawlessly performed in accordance with the Law of Moses, could never take away sins. It did not have the authority nor the power. **It could not remove guilt**. This is the meaning of "no more conscience of sins" and no "remembrance...of sins every year".

One component of perfection is the taking away of sins. This is in keeping with the New Covenant of Jer 31:34 and Heb 8:12 which tell us that God will not remember their sins.

The atoning limitations of animal sacrifices shed light on the meaning of perfect. Heb 10:1-4 is a reference to the yearly Day of Atonement found in Leviticus and Numbers. Aaron, the high priest, was required to offer a bullock and a goat for a sin offering. The results of that day are found in Lev 16:30.

> "For on that day shall the priest make an atonement for you, to cleanse you, that ye may be clean from all your sins before the LORD." Lev 16:30

Because it occurred yearly, we know this was a temporary "cleansing". Heb 10:4 tells us that "atonement", "cleanse" nor "clean" could not mean their sins were taken away. All this time they were temporarily "passed over" (Rom 3:25). Also, the word "forgiven" found in certain Levitical verses (Lev 4:20; 5:10; 6:7 and 19:22) had a temporary meaning because these sacrifices were repeated daily, monthly and yearly as an "atonement for his sins".

Nevertheless, though forgiveness was temporary, it was still a blessing because various verses found in Leviticus tell us that God experienced a "sweet savour" regarding these animal sacrifices. The more "weightier matters", namely obedience and faith, pleases God in any age. Suffice it to say that God was using the Law of Moses to teach multiple lessons to the Israelites.

In the next chapter, we will expand upon the relationship between perfection, justification and the taking away of sins.

"a body hast thou prepared me"

> "But this man, after he had offered one sacrifice for sins for ever, sat down on the right hand of God;" Heb 10:12

God understood what had to be done in order to save a sinful world. Either the world dies or Christ dies. Such is the significance of "one sacrifice for sins for ever".

> "But we see Jesus, who was made a little lower than the angels for the suffering of death, crowned with glory and honour; that he by the grace of God should taste death for every man." Heb 2:9

Thank God for His grace!

The death and resurrection of Christ had been planned from the very beginning.

> "Forasmuch as ye know that ye were…redeemed…with the precious blood of Christ…Who verily was foreordained before the foundation of the world, but was manifest in these last times for you," 1Pet 1:18-20

With the death, resurrection and the appointment of Christ as high priest the types have been relegated to their rightful place. They have not been totally eliminated for they can instruct and teach us and according to Jeremiah will have a future role in Christ's kingdom.

> "Now all these things happened unto them for ensamples: and they are written for our admonition, upon whom the ends of the world are come." 1Cor 10:11

> "For whatsoever things were written aforetime were written for our learning, that we through patience and comfort of the scriptures might have hope." Rom 15:4

Conclusion:

Four key words are found in the Heb 9:11-15 passage: high priest, tabernacle, mediator and New Covenant. But of the four, the Partakers were directed toward Christ only as the high priest. See Heb 2:17; 4:14, 15; 6:20; 7:24, 25; 8:1.

In the future, Christ will be one with those who completed the race once the New Covenant has been established. But in the present, dealing with their sins was their biggest need as they laboured "to enter into that rest" (Heb 4:11; 12:1).

That the New Covenant had not been established on the earth is confirmed by a cursory reading of Jer 31:33, 34 or Heb 8:10-12. The Old Covenant, though fading, was still active at the time Hebrews was written. See Heb 8:4, 13. The two covenants could not exist on the earth at the same time.

1) Christ's shed blood redeemed the world unto God (Heb 2:9; 2Cor 5:15, 18).
2) Christ's shed blood was necessary to fulfill the "promise of eternal inheritance".
3) Christ's shed blood was the blood of the New Covenant (Matt 26:28).
4) Paul emphasized the redemptive authority of Christ's blood.
5) The blood of animals was a type and could not take away sins.
6) Only Christ's death could eliminate the "power of death" (Heb 2:14).
7) God planned Christ's crucifixion from the very beginning.
8) The types taught that the removal of the guilt of sin required the shedding of blood.
9) Only Christ's blood could permanently deal with the guilt of sin.
10) Before Christ shed His blood, God "passed over" Old Covenant sins (Rom 3:25).
11) The Partakers had access to Christ as High Priest.
12) However, they did not yet have access to Christ as the mediator of the New Covenant.

"A Better Covenant"

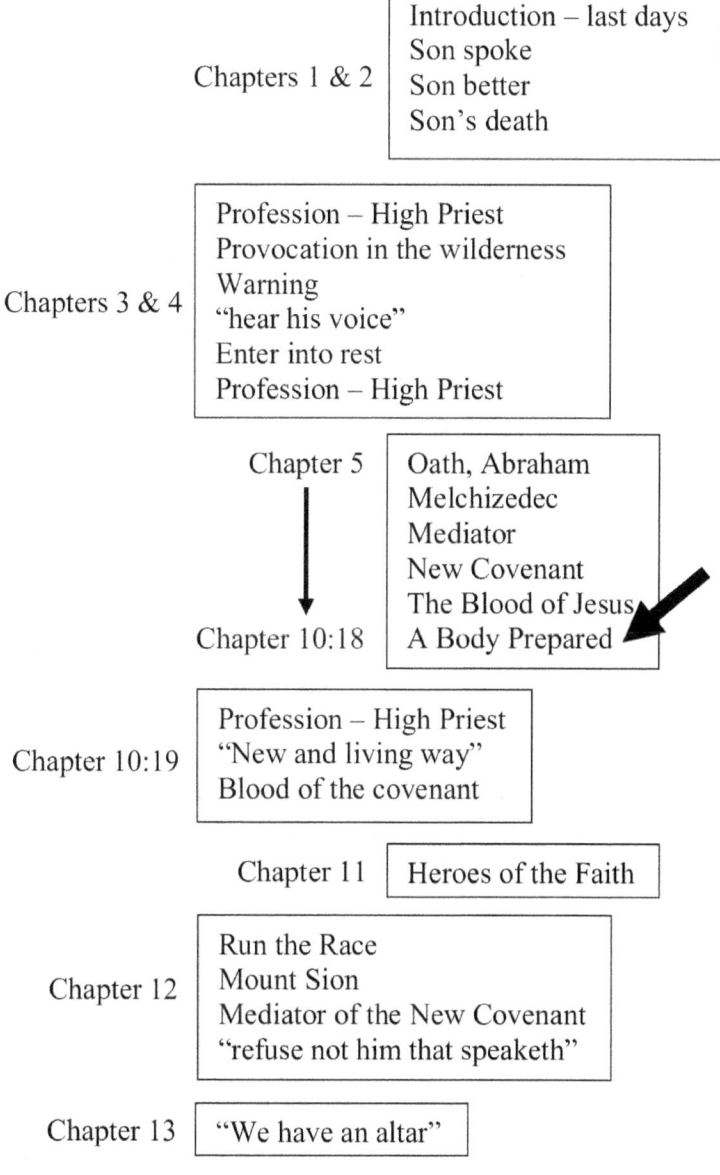

CHAPTER 10

Perfection

QuickTake:

> The taking away of sins is closely associated with justification and perfection – neither of which was attainable by the Law. In this chapter, the connection of these two words is examined by comparing the gospel of the Body of Christ to that of the Partakers. A universal roadmap leading to eternal life is presented. It links certain keywords applicable to everybody regardless of the time period.

Several Greek words are translated into our English word perfect. However, the general sense in the Greek is to finish, to complete the performance of an activity. The context defines what the state of completion will look like. The following verses demonstrate the different meanings.

It can mean **absolute** perfection such as in Matt 5:48.
Surprisingly, it can mean **mending** as in Matt 4:21.
It can mean **full age** as in Heb 5:14 - typically translated mature in other translations.
It can mean **fulfilled** or **finished** as in Luke 2:43 or John 17:4.

However, the definition we are interested in is linked with sins taken away; where there is no remembrance of sins; where there is no more conscience of sins, and therefore, no more guilt of sin. (Heb 10:1-4).

For Adam's descendants, no higher pinnacle can be reached during our days on earth than to have God impute His righteousness to us. While inheritance can be guaranteed, it cannot be obtained or appointed to us in our natural, earthy bodies. Why not? Because

> "**...flesh and blood** cannot inherit the kingdom of God; neither doth corruption inherit incorruption." 1Cor 15:50

That's the reason the Holy Spirit was given as a guarantee of inheritance to members of the Body of Christ. Note the wording in Eph 1:13, 14.

> "In whom ye also trusted, after that ye heard the word of truth, the gospel of your salvation: in whom also after that ye believed, ye were sealed with that holy Spirit of promise,
>
> Which is the earnest of our inheritance until the redemption of the purchased possession, unto the praise of his glory." Eph 1:13, 14

The word earnest denotes a pledge or guarantee. As long as we exist in "flesh and blood" inheritance is not possible. So God gives us, members of the Body of Christ, the next best thing: He imputes His righteousness onto us, thereby guaranteeing the promise of eternal inheritance.

So while we members of the Body of Christ are righteous, we do not have perfection.

How does righteousness tie in with perfection? Heb 10:1, 4 connected the taking away of sins with the word perfect. Being declared righteous has the same result. After God declares a "flesh and blood" sinner righteous, his sins are not counted against him. His sins have been remitted. They have been taken away – fully taken away. Note Rom 4:6-8.

> "Even as David also describeth the blessedness of the man, unto whom God **imputeth righteousness** without works,
>
> Saying, Blessed are they whose iniquities are forgiven, and whose sins are covered.
>
> Blessed is the man to whom the **Lord will not impute sin**." Rom 4:6-8

This passage is very instructive for it tells us that the blessing of righteousness results in the elimination of sin counted against the believer. The passage does not say that those who have been counted righteous will not sin. It states that those who have been counted righteous do not have sin counted against them.

Did all believers in Paul's day possess God's righteousness? No – only members of the Body of Christ; only the died-with-Christ believers. This term will be explained below. In contrast to the members of the Body of Christ in Paul's day, the blessing of righteousness had not been bestowed upon the had-not-died believers to whom the book of Hebrews was addressed. Rather, they were exhorted to "labour" toward that blessing.

Comparison and Contrast

We will deviate somewhat to show a comparison/contrast of salvation between the Body of Christ and the Partakers of Hebrews. It will demonstrate (1) the sin-not-counted significance of imputed righteousness and (2) the specific timing (the "when") that justification was imputed and to whom.

The two figures below illustrate sinners transitioning from under sin to righteousness. Figure 2 takes its title from Heb 3:1. In view of Heb 2:1-4, the "partakers of the heavenly calling" were doctrinally aligned with the Four Gospels, Pentecost and early Acts. This is key in order to understand the difference between the two groups of believers.

The left and right sides of the two figures are the same. The difference is in the middle – describing how **the sinner's sin is dealt with**.

Consider the following figures. Figure 1 is presented below, while Figure 2 is on the following page.

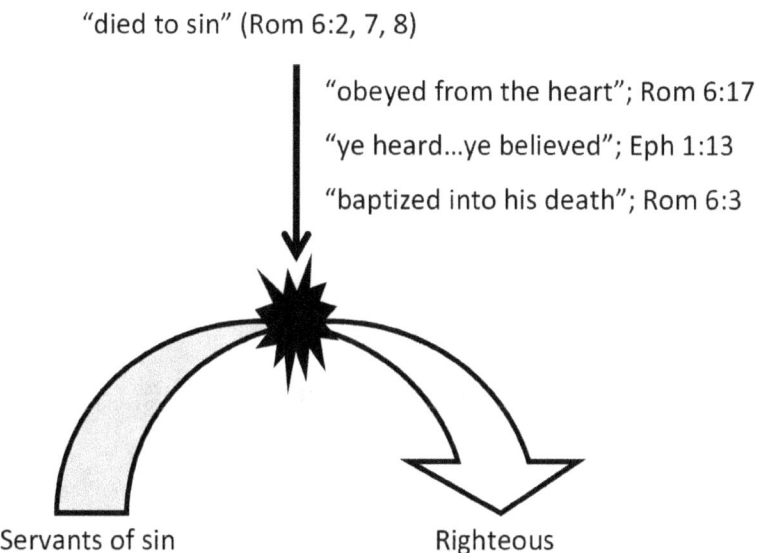

Figure 1 - Body of Christ

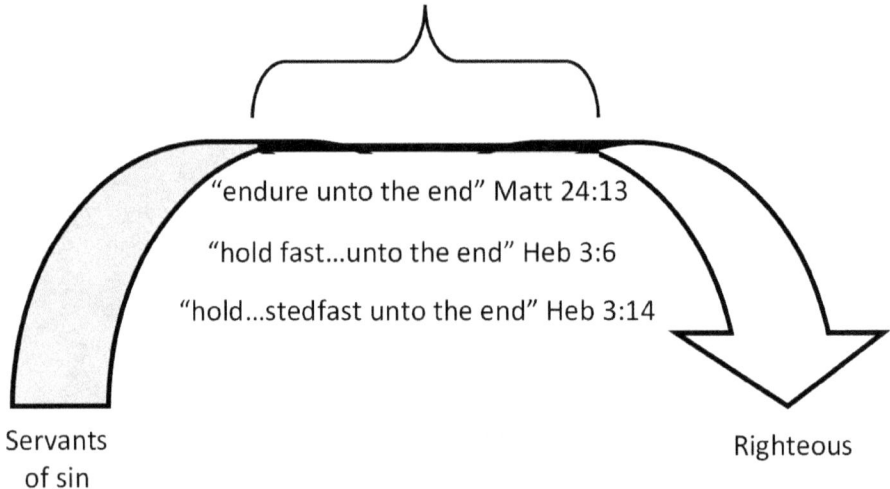

Figure 2 – Partakers of the Heavenly Calling

Before we discuss the figures, a brief background is helpful.

> "As it is written, there is none righteous, no, not one:" Rom 3:10

> "And have hope toward God, which they themselves also allow, that there shall be a resurrection of the dead, both of the just and unjust." Acts 24:15

Rom 3:10 reminds us everybody is unrighteous from birth. However, Acts 24:15 tells us that some will be resurrected as just (righteous). Those who had the righteousness of faith bestowed upon them will be included in the just. Having God's righteousness imputed to a person is the greatest event that could ever happen in life.

The five Bible characters below received God's righteousness; same end result. However, the means (the thing they did or the message believed), was different from one another.

Abel offered an excellent sacrifice – Heb 11:4
Noah prepared an ark - Heb 11:7
Abram believed his seed would number as the stars – Gen 15:5, 6
Phinehas executed judgment – Psa 106:29-31
Rahab received the spies – Heb 11:31

In Figures 1 and 2 the term "servant of sin" is taken from Rom 6:17, 20. According to Rom 6:20 a servant of sin is free from righteousness. And since all of Adam's descendants were born unrighteous, all of us started out as servants of sin; the left side of Figures 1 and 2. This is true of the five Bible characters above.

It's important we don't confuse activities of obedience (Abel, Noah, Rahab, and Phinehas above) for works. Works exalt the sinner. Faith exalts God. In the examples above, all five sinners were justified by the "righteousness of faith" even though most "DID something". This "DID something" should not be confused as works. See the footnote at the end of the chapter for a brief definition of works and grace.

The section entitled **The Road to Eternal Life**, at the end of this chapter, examines this subject more fully.

Figure 1

Gospel: Christ died for our sins.

Figure 1 applies today and applied to members of the body of Christ in Paul's day. All the action occurs at the starburst. The starburst denotes the instant the sinner believed the gospel, having heard God's good news. After the sinner believes the gospel, he is immediately placed into the Body of Christ. What specifically happened to him during the transition? Rom 6:17, 18 inform us.

> "But God be thanked, that ye were the servants of sin, but ye have obeyed from the heart that form of doctrine which was delivered you."
>
> "Being then made free from sin, ye became the servants of righteousness." Rom 6:17, 18

In the language of Rom 6, having heard the gospel, the believing sinner obeyed. The arrow points to the starburst – the point of obedience. At the very instant the sinner obeyed, his old man died and he rose from the dead with Christ as a NEW CREATURE. And exactly at that very moment, God imputed His righteousness unto him. This all occurred at the blink of an eye!

Rom 6:18 describes the sequence of two events: The first event was "Being then made free from sin". The second event was "became the servants of righteousness".

Consider the first event. How did believing the gospel make the sinner free from sin? Three verses from Rom 6 tell us.

> "let it not be! **we who died** to the sin -- how shall we still live in it?" Rom 6:2 (YLT)
>
> "...so many of us as were baptized into Jesus Christ were **baptized into his death**..." Rom 6:3
>
> "for he who **hath died** hath been set free from the sin." Rom 6:7 (YLT).

The instant you believed the Gospel of the Grace of God - the very moment you "obeyed from the heart" - you died with Christ at the cross. Yes, it was a spiritual death but a very real one nonetheless.

But God also counted you as having been buried and risen with Christ (Rom 6:4). The risen you has "put on Christ" – Gal 3:27

> "For as many of you as have been baptized into Christ have put on Christ." Gal 3:27

Those that have died and risen with Christ - that have "put on Christ" - have taken on all the blessings which are in Christ. One such blessing was the imputation of God's righteousness. The risen you that came out of the grave is the New Man – a new creation being neither Jew or Gentile - upon whom God declared His righteousness (Rom 3:22; Eph 4:24).

> "Even the righteousness of God which is by faith of Jesus Christ unto all and upon all them that believe: for there is no difference:" Rom 3:22

> "And that ye put on the new man, which after God is created in righteousness and true holiness." Eph 4:24

The reader is strongly encouraged to study Eph 1:13, 14 where we learn the believing sinner was "**sealed** with that holy Spirit of promise, Which is the earnest *[guarantee]* of our inheritance."

We conclude that righteousness was imputed to the members of the Body of Christ because they were fully identified with Christ. This was brought about because members of the Body of Christ died and resurrected with Christ.

Summary: Today, the **believing sinner deals with his sins by dying with Christ** at the INSTANT OF BELIEVING. Having died with Christ, the sinner is freed from sin. It follows that the believing sinner rises with Christ and, as a result, has "put on Christ" (Gal 3:27). And since Christ is righteous, we also are righteous being one with Him. (See Rom 6:8; 8:17; Gal 2:20; Eph 2:5; Col 3:1, 3).

Question: How did the sinner deal with his sin?
Answer: The sinner submitted to the demands of sin: he **DIED**. He died with Christ. He was baptized into Christ's death.

Figure 2

Gospel: Kingdom of Heaven at hand; Jesus of Nazareth is King, Lord and Christ.

Notice there is no starburst in the middle. The big difference here is that there is no significant, single salvation event in the middle. The "instant of believing" was not applicable to the Partakers as it was to the members of the Body of Christ. Rather than a single, significant point, they must run a race. It is a journey.

> "Wherefore seeing we also are compassed about with so great a cloud of witnesses, let us lay aside every weight, and the sin which doth so easily beset us, and **let us run with patience the race that is set before us**," Heb 12:1

Two questions: (1) what did the Partakers have to do in order to have God impute His righteousness unto them; in order to achieve perfection? And (2) when does that occur? The answer is found in the middle, which explains how the sinner deals with his sin. In Figure 1, the sinner dealt with his sin by dying to sin. But, not so in Figure 2.

What was the primary message of the gospel the Partakers believed? This is easily answered by examining the gospel the nation of Israel heard at Pentecost. Why Pentecost? Because, per Heb 2:1 4, the Partakers are doctrinally aligned/united with Peter's message in early Acts.
Peter's message to Israel did not include "Christ died for our sins". Rather, it was "Christ died **because** of your sins - your wickedness"! Peter was not presenting Christ's death as the divine solution to the sin problem. Quite the contrary, Israel was charged with the murder of Christ! (Acts 2:23, 36; 3:14, 15; 4:10, 11; 5:30; 7:52). The reader is strongly encouraged to read each of these eight verses. It is very enlightening.

Those who repented and were baptized in early Acts became believers. But note, they were not died-with-Christ believers. And since they had not died, they had not resurrected from the dead. Not having resurrected, they had not been "baptized into Christ" and thus, had not "put on Christ". And note carefully, they were not new creatures after they believed.

The Difference: Members of the Body of Christ died with the Lord. The believers at Pentecost, as well as the Partakers, did not.

To the point, the Partakers in Hebrews had not (at the time of the writing of Hebrews) been declared righteous. That is what they were racing toward. We believe they will attain God's righteousness when they finally "enter into his rest". But, at the time Hebrews was written, the exhortation/warning was to

> "...**labour** therefore to enter into that rest, lest any man fall after the same example of unbelief." Heb 4:11

Figure 2 illustrates one component of the "labour". It is taken from Heb 2:17

> "Wherefore in all things it behoved him to be made like unto his brethren, that he might be a merciful and faithful high priest in things pertaining to God, to make **reconciliation for the sins of the people**." Heb 2:17

Hebrews was written to exhort the wavering Partakers to continue running the race. The overall context suggests they started well but were seemingly reverting back to the Mosaic Law in order to approach God. Through various comparisons and contrasts, the author demonstrated that Christ's priesthood was the substance, while Moses, Aaron and the Levitical priesthood had been types from the very beginning. Central to this is that Christ's blood is the only blood with the authority and power to "take away sins" (Heb 10:11, 12). And, in contrast to the Levitical sacrifices, it was shed one time and one time only!

According to the Mosaic Law when the Israelite sinned, he was instructed to bring an animal to the tabernacle as a sacrifice in order to atone for that sin (Lev 1-5). After killing the animal, the blood was taken by the Levitical priest and applied to the altar. The priest performed his duty on behalf of the Israelite. It was a propitiation for his sin. The worshipper was making "reconciliation for the sins of" himself.

But now (several years after Pentecost), the Partaker had knowledge of the reality of Christ's priesthood and of the impotency of the Mosaic Law. So, going forward, when he sinned, the Partaker would "enter into the holiest by the blood of Jesus" (Heb 10:19). Yes, it was a spiritual entrance but a very real one nonetheless. He would not dare bring the blood of an animal to an impotent priest expecting a forever forgiveness!

Christ had done it all. The repentant Partaker – acknowledging that the real blood had already been shed - need only present himself to the real High Priest. We believe this is the meaning of 1John 1:9, 10

> "If we confess our sins, he is faithful and just to forgive us our sins, and to cleanse us from all unrighteousness.
>
> If we say that we have not sinned, we make him a liar, and his word is not in us." 1John 1:9, 10

Summary: The Partaker was in a race where he was to patiently "labour...to enter into that rest". God invited him to "come boldly", "lay hold", "draw nigh" and "come unto" the throne of grace where the "merciful and faithful high priest" would deal with his sins. He was to leave the shadow system behind and embrace the real high priest. And most importantly, he was to offer Christ's already shed blood. That blood and that blood only would appease God.

Question: How did the sinner deal with his sin?
Answer: The sinner acknowledged his sin ("confess our sins") and sought reconciliation of those sins by entering the holiest to meet with Christ the high priest – with Christ's blood "in hand". In order to have his sin taken away, he placed his trust (1) on the once-shed blood of Christ and (2) on the intercessory authority of Jesus Christ as the one and only high priest of God. As often as he sinned, he entered the holiest for the "reconciliation of his sin". He would do this as often as needed during the race.

Road to Eternal Life

Regardless of who God has dealt with in the Bible, one standard has never changed: righteousness or justification is always by faith – not of works.* A sinner, under the rightful condemnation of God's divine law, has no standing before a Holy God. He is not in any position to make his case to God with his noble activities or ideas. He is not in any position to strike a deal or negotiate with God. The only thing he is in a position to do is die. He was found guilty and sentenced to die by God's standard – the Law.

However, out of mercy, grace and love, God graciously extends, as a gift, eternal life to the condemned-to-die sinner who expresses faith and obedience in the particular message that God is communicating to him. Regardless of the message, the "roadmap" is the same and applies to all mankind throughout human history. The roadmap below, formed by linking 6 verses, illustrates the connection of keywords we have heard all of our lives. The verse with the large star marks man's entrance into eternal life.

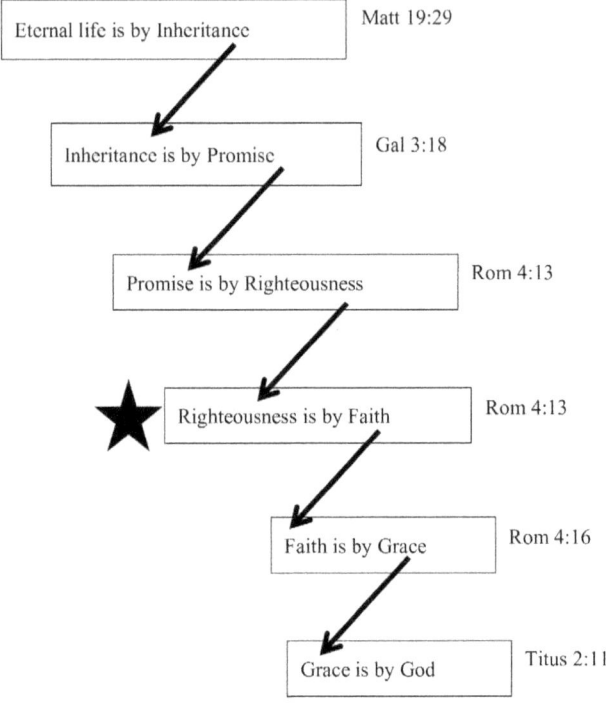

There are a couple of side roads that are significant. Inheritance is in the form of sonship and sonship, as defined by the Bible, is by resurrection.

> "for they cannot even die anymore, because they are like angels, and are sons of God, being sons of the resurrection." Luke 20:36 (NASB95)

> "who was declared the Son of God with power by the resurrection from the dead..." Rom 1:4 (NASB95)

Even though Rom 4:13 and Gal 3:18 make it clear that neither promise nor inheritance is of the Law, the Law is not at odds with either of them.

> "Is the law then against the promises of God? God forbid: for if there had been a law given which could have given life, verily righteousness should have been by the law." Gal 3:21

The purpose of the Law was the "knowledge of sin". It was to convince the unrighteous of their sinfulness, and thus point them to God and His mercy (Luke 18:13). It was never intended to result in righteousness. As long as we don't mix up the objectives of grace and the Law, we will not get confused.

A Point of Clarification

Righteousness has always been by faith. But, as we have seen with the 5 Bible characters, God may deal with one person quite differently from another. God may want one person to "do nothing". He may want another to "do something". Note the following example from 1John,

Demonstrating hate will be catastrophic. They will have to show love to the brethren (an example of the "do something" people). The admonition of 1John 3:14, 15 is clearly addressed to "my brethren".

> "We know that we have passed from death unto life, because we love the brethren. He that loveth not his brother abideth in death.
>
> Whosoever hateth his brother is a murderer: and ye know that no murderer hath eternal life abiding in him." 1John 3:14, 15

Carefully read these verses. Note that these brethren did not have the assurance of eternal security. Whether or not they would receive eternal life depended on whether they hated or loved! These passages are discussed in detail in my second book DIED WITH CHRIST.

Also, the timing may be different. For Abram and the Body of Christ, righteousness was imputed immediately upon believing. But that does not mean it is true of all people. Some people will have to "endure unto the end" to "be saved" (Matt 10:22; 24:13).

Stumblingstone

As Gentiles, we may not fully comprehend the strong bond that Israelites of that time had to the Law of Moses. It was their life. It was their identity which set them apart from the rest of the world. It connected them, and them alone, to the one true God. The bulk of the Scriptures was about them and the promises made to them by God.

But their self-promoting misinterpretation of the Law was their downfall. Instead of humility, they exalted themselves (Luke 18:9-12, 14). The deceptive teaching that the Law possessed the ability to impart righteousness through works was the Goliath the author of Hebrews was trying to defeat. For sure, Israel had a zeal for God (Rom 10:2) but they were set upon obtaining righteousness in their own way (Rom 9:30-10:4). It blinded them to the righteousness available in Christ. They had not

> "submitted themselves unto the righteousness of God. For Christ is the end of the law for righteousness to everyone that believeth" Rom 10:3, 4.

What about the Partakers? They had expressed faith in the risen Christ and received confirmation of

> "so great salvation...God...bearing them witness, both with signs and wonders..." Heb 2:3, 4

But they were in jeopardy of coming short of entering into His Rest. Instead of teaching others, they had to be taught again the basic principles (Heb 5:12). The idea that the Law could result in righteousness was so ingrained in their traditions, the author of Hebrews had to devote nearly 40% of the letter convincing the Christ-believers of the impotency of the Law.

Seeking righteousness was proper. But seeking it through the Law was flat-out disobedience and contrary to the Law itself. Moving forward, the author challenged the Partakers to leave

"...the principles of the doctrine of Christ, let us go on unto perfection..." Heb 6:1

Back to the Left Side

Before we transition back and consider the left side of the outline, there are important summary points to remember which we learned from the right side. Heb 10:16-18 give us the overall goal and means of the last five chapters. The goal is the New Covenant found in Heb 10:16, 17 - quoting Jer 31:33, 34. The means is the offering/sacrifice of Christ. So complete was Christ's shed blood that Heb 10:18 describes it as "there is no more offering for sin".

Question: Well, since Christ has shed His blood and it is the blood of the New Covenant, what was keeping the Partakers from enjoying perfect fellowship with God in the promise land? The text from Heb 9:26 to Heb 10:18 gives us indications that much remained to be done. Chapter 4 of this book, "But Now We See Not", spoke of the "troublous times" to come. Prophecy must take its course – as the following indicates:

1) "...but now once in the **end of the ages**..." Heb 9:26
2) "...them that look for him...appear **the second time**..." Heb 9:28
3) "...in **the scroll** (referring to the Scriptures)...written of me..." Heb 10:7
4) "...He taketh away the **first**...establish the **second**" Heb 10:9
5) "...expecting till his **enemies be made his footstool**" Heb 10:13

These five verses point to the culmination of God's prophetic plan for Israel. Point 5 is especially interesting and is discussed at length in Chapter 13 of this book. But here we see that it fits nicely, at the tail end of events necessary to fulfill Israel's prophetic plan.

Answer: Several events must transpire before the New Covenant is fully realized.

Conclusion:

1) Justification and perfection result in the taking away of sins.
2) "flesh and blood" cannot inherit eternal life.
3) The righteousness-declared sinner has the guarantee of eternal life.
4) Righteousness is imputed at the instant of belief for the Body of Christ.
5) The Partakers must "endure unto the end" to receive justification and inheritance.
6) By seeking righteousness by the works of the Law, Israel stumbled.

*

"Works" has a variety of meanings. But the focus here is the meaning of works as defined in Rom 11:6. It is completely separated from righteousness by faith.

> "And if by grace, then is it no more of works: otherwise grace is no more grace. But if it be of works, then is it no more grace: otherwise work is no more work." Rom 11:6

The works of Rom 11:6 has no association whatsoever to faith. It is the no-more-grace works. A physical activity may or may not be a no-more-grace work. The context will determine that.

The confusion arises because physical acts of obedience and no-more-grace works are most always physical by nature. But one honors God, while the other disregards God's grace and is VOID OF FAITH. Refer to the account of Phinehas in Num 25 for an example of a physical activity, which honored God. It was an act of obedience – clearly NOT a no-more-grace work.

Some characteristics of the Rom 11:6 no-more-grace works are:

1) "of their own hands" Acts 7:41
2) "that of yourselves" Eph 2:8
3) "works of the Law" Rom 3:20
4) "man should boast" Eph 2:9
5) "reckoned...of debt" Rom 4:4 (earnings)

Perfection

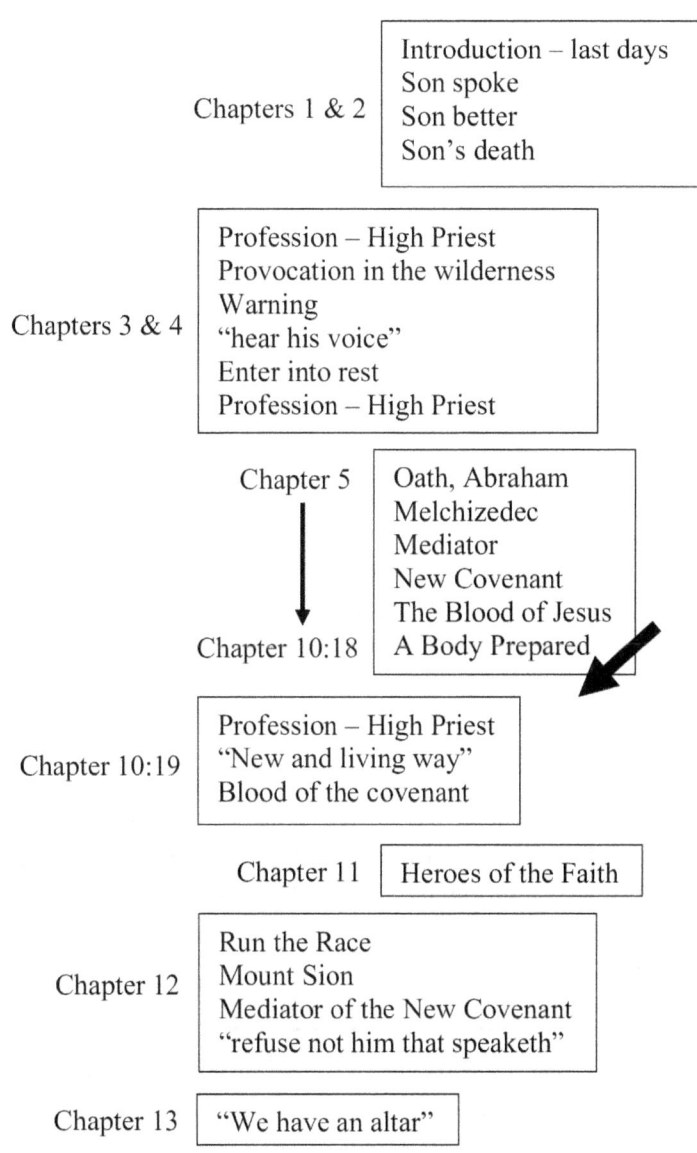

CHAPTER 11

"The Profession of our Faith"

QuickTake:

> Having received the "knowledge of the truth", the Partakers were now emboldened to continue the race with confidence. But with knowledge comes responsibility and accountability. The author gave his readers stern words not to waver from their profession.

In previous chapters we have written about Christ as high priest, His blood, the New Covenant and perfection. So before we proceed, let's relate Christ's office of high priest with Christ as the mediator of the New Covenant. We have stated that, though Christ's blood had been shed and Christ had been appointed mediator, the New Covenant had not been realized at least not on earth (Heb 8:4). Thus, the Partakers were not exhorted to seek out Christ as mediator of the New Covenant. It was still future. Conversely, the Partakers were clearly and repeatedly exhorted to seek out Christ as high priest. Why the high priest and not the mediator? Because sin was still at the forefront. It was the issue (Heb 2:17; 3:13; 10:26, 29; 12:1). Perfection and righteousness will follow after God is completely propitiated and His prophetic plan is fully implemented. Perfection will be conferred as the New Covenant is established with the believers declared righteous.

Refer to the outline in the previous page. In this chapter we will return to the left side of the outline. You'll recall that the indentations separated the book of Hebrews into two major portions: (1) Those that generally comprised of historical or doctrinal information intended for the consideration of the Partakers (right side) and (2) those that were speaking directly to the Partakers - reproofs, encouragements, exhortations intended as reassurances to run the race (left side).

First comes knowledge, followed by action in line with that knowledge.

The right indentations centered about Christ's priesthood. Since Christ as high priest was not found anywhere in the Bible, the author of Hebrews devoted a sizeable percentage in order to convince his readers of the legitimacy, authority and the advantages of the priesthood of Christ.

And having succeeded in doing so, we believe the author returns to the primary subject of Hebrews - "profession of our faith". Heb 10:19 picks up where Chapter 4 left off. The flow of thought in these two passages is apparent when observed as a sequence.

> Seeing then that we have a great high priest, that is passed into the heavens, Jesus the Son of God, let us hold fast our profession.
>
>> Let us therefore come boldly unto the throne of grace, that we may obtain mercy, and find grace to help in time of need." Heb 4:14, 16
>>
>> Having therefore, brethren, boldness to enter into the holiest by the blood of Jesus,
>
> Let us hold fast the profession of our faith without wavering; (for he is faithful that promised;)" Heb 10:19, 23

We encourage the reader to review the summary of "our profession" found in page fifty five of this book.

A Line in the Sand

The passage from Heb 10:12 to 10:18 forms a summary of the last five chapters of Hebrews – and can be described by our Lord's words on the cross "It is finished". The opening word of Heb 10:12, **But**, draws a distinct "line in the sand".

On one side of the line is the ineffective blood of animals and the impotent Levitical priests (Heb 10:4, 11). Both are described as not able to "take away sins". The Law's inability to permanently remove sin had been gradually revealed throughout their 1500 years of history; for which God graciously made allowances (Rom 3:25). The Law had its purpose. But making the worshippers perfect was not one of them.

On the other side of the line is the finished work of Christ, which did "take away sins". And because of the completeness and finality of His work, Heb 10:18 concludes

> "Now where remission of these is, there is no more offering for sin." Heb 10:18

"No more offering for sins" - this formed the "don't-look-back" truth as the Partakers continued to run the race. The blood of the New Covenant had been shed. Only those who come with "blood in hand" and enter into the holiest would take part in its ratification.

Heb 10:19-23 forms the apex of the letter.

Before that, the Partakers had been schooled with the truth of Christ, His superior priesthood and His efficacious shed blood. But now that they had "received the *[full]* knowledge of the truth" and were reminded again "…there remaineth no more sacrifice for sins" (Heb 10:26), they were given the strongest warning in the epistle.

God had resurrected Jesus of Nazareth from the dead, declared Him Son and heir, placed Him at His right hand and appointed Him high priest. To go back to animal sacrifices would be to disregard the entire redemptive work of God, the Son and the Holy Spirit.

Heb 10:29 described such a person as one

> "…who hath trodden under foot the Son of God, and hath counted the blood of the covenant, wherewith he was sanctified, an unholy thing, and hath done despite unto the Spirit of grace? Heb 10:29

A person who displayed total disregard for the blood that ratified the covenant, had no reverence for the covenant itself. That contempt demonstrated a desertion of "the profession of our faith".

"Sin Wilfully"

> "For if we sin wilfully after that we have received the knowledge of the truth, there remaineth no more sacrifice for sins," Heb 10:26

What does this mean? The answer is important for the verses which follow speak of a "sorer punishment" at the "hands of the living God". To answer this question, let's briefly review the purpose of the letter.

The author had just completed writing the largest segment of the letter, where the main topic was the priesthood of Christ. In so doing, the Levitical priesthood along with the blood sacrifices of animals were revealed as having no redeeming value at all – none! The wavering Partakers were on the fence with the Levitical system, its priests and animal sacrifices on one side and Christ, the "High Priest of our profession" on the other. They had started well (Heb 10:32-34) and should have been teachers (Heb 5:12) but had become "dull of hearing" and "slothful".

The author, not mixing words, had used strong language admonishing them to "run with patience the race that is set before us".

> "Take heed, brethren, lest there be in any of you an evil heart of unbelief, in departing from the living God.
>
> But exhort one another daily, while it is called To day; lest any of you be hardened through the deceitfulness of sin." Heb 3:12, 13

> "Let us therefore fear, lest, a promise being left us of entering into his rest, any of you should seem to come short of it." Heb 4:1

> "Let us labour therefore to enter into that rest, lest any man fall after the same example of unbelief." Heb 4:11

The word knowledge in Heb 10:26 is *epígnōsis,* which is Strongs #1922. This word is more than knowledge, it is "full knowledge". The use of this word highlights, not just any truth, but the just-revealed truth of Christ's priesthood. This is the specific topic of discussion the author was having with his readers. Naturally, the author would be concerned about sins in general. But in Heb 10:26, his focus was more specific. His main concern throughout the entire epistle had been the possibility of their "departing from the living God". To that point, the author exhorted the Partakers to

> "...hold fast the profession of *our* faith without wavering..." Heb 10:23

Thus, we believe "sin wilfully" specifically refers to the abandonment of Christ's authority and priesthood with its ability to "take away sins" - that which the Levitical system could not do. With the full picture now revealed, they clearly understood there was "no more sacrifice for sins". And how would they show that abandonment? They would regress back to the shadow system - the Law which "made nothing perfect".

Benson explains:

> "...in the former part of the epistle, [*the author*] had proved that the sacrifices of the law were all abolished, and that the only sacrifice for sin remaining was the sacrifice of Christ, it followed that apostates, who willfully renounced the benefit of that sacrifice, had no sacrifice for sin whatever remaining to them."
> *Joseph Benson Commentary on the Old and New Testaments*

Eternal Security?

Even the casual student of the Scriptures is aware of the "Once Saved, Always Saved" (OSAS) controversy centered about the passages of Heb 6:4-6 and Heb 10:26-31. We will not go into a deep, micro-explanation of certain words and verb tenses to make a point one way or the other – all major viewpoints are amply represented online. Rather, we will provide an overview and a less complicated solution for the reader's consideration. For the record, I am a proponent of OSAS for members of the Body of Christ.

Note three observations:

1) The majority of Christian church-goers assume (a) that all New Testament books, including the book of Hebrews, apply **directly** to members of the Body of Christ; and (b) that OSAS is a false teaching.
2) Generally, the opponents of OSAS take an offensive stance regarding the Hebrew passages.
3) While, the proponents of OSAS take a defensive stance regarding the same Hebrew passages.

By an offensive stance, we mean the Hebrews passages are taken at face value - "it means what it says". And the words of Heb 6 and 10, to their way of thinking, clearly do not support eternal security. This is a very powerful position, which does not require deep thinking – just read and accept the words. On the other hand, the defensive stance attempts to explain why "it means what it says" does not apply to the Heb 6 and 10 passages. Their explanation centers around two primary methods shown below.

(1) **Redefine the words**:
Supporters of this method believe the passages mean something else other than what they say. They don't deny the content of the Hebrew passages in Heb 6 and 10, but hold that they really mean something else. **Their position: The Partakers are members of the Body of Christ; however the words in Heb 6 and 10 cannot be taken at face value.**

(2) **Redefine the people**:
Supporters of this method believe the Hebrews were a mix of members of the Body of Christ and "tasters" (Heb 6:4, 5) – "nominal believers" as one commentator described them. Heb 6 and 10 were specifically addressed to the "tasters" who did not have OSAS salvation to begin with. One online explanation was "They are intellectually persuaded but spiritually uncommitted". Another explanation is that the passages in

Heb 6 and 10 were warnings to "pretend" believers that they needed to examine themselves before it was too late. **Their position: The words in Heb 6 and 10 can be taken at face value; however the words were addressed only to the "pretend" believers who were among the Partakers. The Partakers were members of the Body of Christ but the "pretend" believers were not.**

So we see that the defensive stance attempts to either (1) redefine the words, not the people or (2) redefine the people, not the words. Both have the purpose of maintaining OSAS in Hebrews. And why? Because they believe in OSAS and they further believe that Hebrews directly applies to the Body of Christ.

Most Christian church-goers, who regard all the New Testament as directly applicable to all believers today (Observation 1), fall under the offensive stance. The vast majority of these church-goers DO NOT support "Once Saved, Always Saved". Whereas, OSAS-believing Evangelical Christians, who think all the New Testament (including Hebrews) applies directly to the Body of Christ, fall under the defensive stance.

In summary, the three main groups are (1) the "it means what it says" Observation 1 group. They do not support OSAS; (2) the "redefine the words" OSAS supporters and (3) the "redefine the people" OSAS supporters. The vast majority of members comprising these three groups generally believe that Hebrews was written to and is about the Body of Christ.

I fall into a very minority fourth group. We are OSAS-believing Christians who DO NOT hold that Hebrews was directly written to or is about the Body of Christ. **My position: The "partakers of the heavenly calling" were not members of the Body of Christ. The words in Heb 6 and 10 can be taken at face value.**

The difference between my position and that of the majority of Christians is they believe the book of Hebrews was written to members of the Body of Christ. We hold they were brethren (Heb 3:12); but not members of the Body of Christ.

The reader will save himself a lot of confusion and error if he comes to understand one important fact: The book of Hebrews, while certainly the word of God, was not written directly to the members of the Body of Christ. And because the Partakers of Hebrews were not members of the Body of Christ, OSAS did not apply to them – they did not have eternal security.

The Solution: Stop trying to force OSAS upon the Partakers. It was not God's plan for them.

It would be helpful to review the difference between the Body of Christ and the Partakers. Refer to Figures 1 and 2 on pages one hundred five and one hundred six.

"things not seen"

The author of Hebrews was keenly aware of the difficulties the Partakers were experiencing as they ran the race set before them. To that end, he offered practical encouragement in two areas: (1) assembling or fellowship and (2) standards.

(1) Assembling:
While they could not see their high priest, they had each other. The author exhorted them to

> "...consider one another to provoke unto love and to good works:
>
> Not forsaking the assembling of ourselves together, as the manner of some is; but exhorting one another: and so much the more, as ye see the day approaching." Heb 10:24, 25

This is very important. Mob mentality is a powerful force, which drives and shapes many negative facets of a society and culture. While it can't be changed, one can certainly separate from it; which is the core of sanctification. Separation has always been a mainstay for God's people.

We readily see how it could have helped the Partakers. They were to separate themselves from the proponents of Judaism and gather with fellow Partakers to

> "...provoke unto love and to good works...exhorting one another..."

(2) Standards:
Chapter 11 is often referred to as "Heroes of the faith". This chapter is about well-known Bible characters the Partakers could relate to. Most of the Heroes lived a fairly rough life in their faithfulness to God. Heb 11:13-16 state

> "These all **died in faith, not having received the promises**, but having seen them afar off, and were persuaded of them, and embraced them, and confessed that they were strangers and pilgrims on the earth.
>
> ...they seek a country.
>
> And truly, if they had been mindful of that country from whence they came out, they might have had opportunity to have returned.
>
> But now they desire a better country, that is, an heavenly: wherefore God is not ashamed to be called their God: for he hath prepared for them a city." Heb 11:13-16

Those that "died in faith, not having received the promises" had higher standards. Returning to the "country from whence they came out" may have meant a more comfortable life. But they kept their minds on something better; even though they never received the promises in their lifetimes.

The jist of Hebrews 11 to the Partakers was "you are not alone". The bulk of God's faithful servants experienced tribulations and persecutions while reaching for a "better country." Heb 12:11 states

"Now no chastening for the present seemeth to be joyous, but grievous: nevertheless afterward it yieldeth the peaceable fruit of righteousness unto them which are exercised thereby." Heb 12:11

Conclusion:

1) The Partakers had received the full knowledge.
2) There was "no more sacrifice for sins".
3) To sin willfully would result in "sorer punishment".
4) Unlike the Body of Christ, the Partakers did not have eternal security.
5) Assembling with other Partakers was paramount.
6) They had each other and the "heroes of the faith" as examples of encouragement.
7) Lowering the standards was not an option.

"The Profession of our Faith"

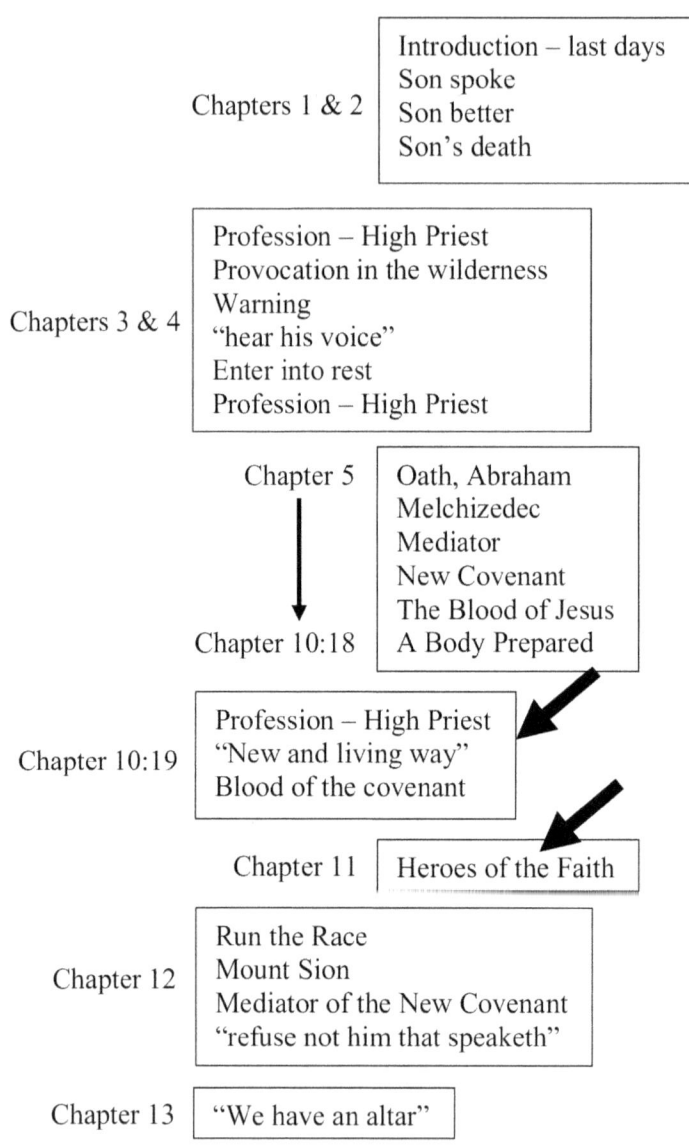

CHAPTER 12

Unfinished Business

QuickTake:

> At Pentecost, the Holy Spirit revealed to Israel Christ as the Prophet of Deut 18. What lay dormant for 1500 years was now before the nation of Israel: "him shall ye hear in all things whatsoever he shall say unto you" (Acts 3:22). Christ spoke God's words to Israel. Now, with His numerous offices and titles known, there was even more reason to "earnest[ly] heed" that "spoken by the Lord" (Heb 2:1-4).

The reference to Mount Sion (Heb 12:22) parallels the reference to Mount Horeb (Deut 18:16). Chapter 5 of this book detailed the origin of the words Jesus spoke while on earth. Recall, Christ stated repeatedly that the words He spoke were "not his", but God's. The point of all that was to remind the nation of Israel that there was unfinished business going all the way back to Exo 20.

God had not forgotten the events of Exo 20:18, 19 when Israel said "Let me not hear again the voice of the LORD my God..." (Deut 18:16). Approximately 40 years later, God responded

> "I will raise them up a Prophet from among their brethren, like unto thee, and will put my words in his mouth; and he shall speak unto them all that I shall command him.
>
> And it shall come to pass, that whosoever will not hearken unto my words which he shall speak in my name, I will require it of him." Deut 18: 18, 19

Approximately 1500 years later, Peter stood up at Pentecost announcing to Israel that the time of The Prophet had arrived.

> "For Moses truly said unto the fathers, a prophet shall the Lord your God raise up unto you of your brethren, like unto me; him shall ye hear in all things whatsoever he shall say unto you.
>
> And it shall come to pass, that every soul, which will not hear that prophet, shall be destroyed from among the people." Acts 3:22, 23

And if there were any doubts what the "I will require it of him" in Deut 18:19 meant, it was dispelled with the words "destroyed from among the people".

With that background, the parallel of Deut 18 with Hebrews 12 becomes apparent. Back then, it was the refusal to hear God. Would the Partakers repeat the error of their fathers? Would they refuse to hear God's words as "spoken unto us by his Son" (Heb 1:2)?

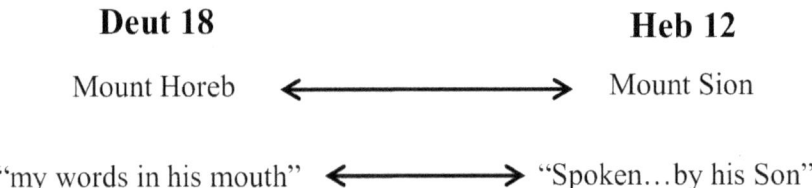

Deut 18   **Heb 12**

Mount Horeb ⟵⟶ Mount Sion

"my words in his mouth" ⟵⟶ "Spoken…by his Son"

God wanted Israel to know, in no uncertain terms, that the words of Christ in the Four Gospels and early Acts were "my words which he shall speak in my name" of Deut 18:19. Peter, in Acts 3:22, 23 could not have been any clearer.

But God, rich in mercy and grace, does not want to punish but bestow blessings. From Heb 12:22 to 25, the author listed eight blessings: beginning with Mount Sion and concluding with the blood of sprinkling. These blessings were intended to encourage the Partakers to finish the race.

But God is also a God of justice. So the author, using the rebellion at Mount Horeb as a background, gave his final warning in Heb 12:25, 26:

> "See that ye refuse not him that speaketh. For if they escaped not who refused him that spake on earth, much more shall not we escape, if we turn away from him that speaketh from heaven:
>
> Whose voice then shook the earth: but now he hath promised, saying, yet once more I shake not the earth only, but also heaven." Heb 12:25, 26

A Word About Birthdays

As was detailed in Chapter 5 of this book, God spoke only to the nation of Israel in Horeb. Gentiles were not present nor were they invited/included. Therefore, the five pronouns in the verses below point to Israel - and to Israel alone.

> "I will raise **them** up a Prophet from among **their** brethren, like unto thee, and will put my words in his mouth; and he shall speak unto **them** all that I shall command him.
>
> And it shall come to pass, that **whosoever** will not hearken unto my words which he shall speak in my name, I will require it of **him**." Deut 18:18, 19

The significance is twofold:

(1) Since, after 1500 years, Peter (Acts 3:22, 23) revealed the identity and arrival of The Prophet, Pentecost is not the "birthday" of the Church, the Body of Christ where "there is neither Jew or Greek..." (Gal 3:28).

Pentecost is not the start of something new. Rather, it is the finale of a 1500-year-old promise made by God to a selective group of people regarding a very specific point of contention.

(2) Since the author of Hebrews exhorted his readers to "give the more earnest heed to the things…spoken by the Lord…" (Heb 2:1, 3), the Partakers were doctrinally attached to the Four Gospels and early Acts. Thus the book of Hebrews, like early Acts, is targeted specifically to the nation of Israel. Like any of the 66 books of the Bible, Hebrews provides members of the Body of Christ with "…doctrine…reproof…correction…" and "…instruction in righteousness" (2Tim 3:16). However, the book of Hebrews was not directly addressed to nor was it about the Body of Christ.

"We have an altar"

The Partakers had a far better altar; one "established with grace", Heb 13:9. However, they could neither touch it nor see it. And that would prove difficult for some. The senses are temporary but their pull is very powerful.

Worship in Judaism, like some Christian denominations, had a strong appeal to the senses. It had the Levitical ministers and the priests with their ornate clothing. The tabernacle with its symbolic specifications had a strong presence. The blood, repeatedly shed, was warm to the touch and very visual – its red color stood out among the furniture in the tabernacle. One can also imagine the smell of blood – a very unique odor which transitions to a stench after some period.

But it was all a type having no real substance other than teaching the Israelite about the infinite gap between himself and God. Its primary purpose was to demonstrate the inability of sinful man. Following the example of the Publican in Luke 18, the discerning Israelite would give up on himself and place all his trust in a merciful God. Ironically, the most valuable lesson learned was that the majestic, Levitical system never could provide any access at all. It could not do anything to remove the vail of separation.

This may not seem like a big deal to today's readers. But, back in that day, with one's family and culture steep in Judaism, it was a force to be reckoned with. Christians who come from a large, devout, religious family can relate to this.

Altar points to worship. The Partakers were to worship, not in Jerusalem, but "unto him without the camp". The "continuing city...one to come" refers to the rebuilt Jerusalem which is part of the "everlasting covenant" of Heb 13:20. See pages seventy three and seventy four. And how were the Partakers to worship? Heb 13:15, 16 gave them familiar commands.

> "By him therefore let us offer the sacrifice of praise to God continually, that is, the fruit of our lips giving thanks to his name." Heb 13:15

> "But to do good and to communicate forget not: for with such sacrifices God is well pleased." Heb 13:16

Heb 13:15 emphasizes "love the Lord thy God". While Heb 13:16 emphasizes "love thy neighbour as thyself"; Mark 12:30, 31. How fitting that Hebrews closed on this note. It's as if the author had challenged the Partakers to get "back to basics". Those that wanted to embrace the Law now had a way to do so.

> "And thou shalt love the LORD thy God with all thine heart, and with all thy soul, and with all thy might." Deut 6:5

Unfinished Business

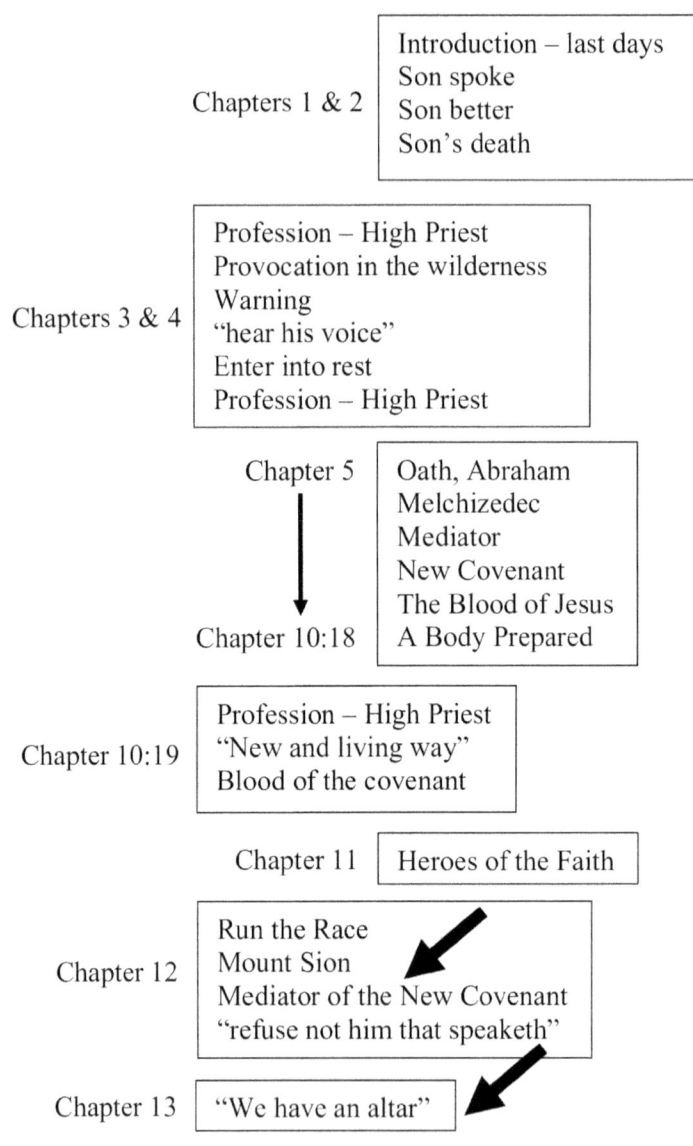

CHAPTER 13

Odds and Ends

QuickTake:

> In our last chapter, we will address some of the difficult passages - not all is black and white. Many truths remain hidden. But we are confident that those truths, though not apparent to us, are in the word of God. We just have to stay diligent.

What was the relationship between the risen Christ and Saul of Tarsus? Simply, that instead of predictably destroying him according to prophecy (Acts 3:23), Christ surprisingly and suddenly spared him. And incredibly, Christ **immediately** conferred a ministry upon Saul: "But rise, and stand upon thy feet...a minister" (Acts 26:16).

Paul described his salvation to Timothy:

> "This is a faithful saying, and worthy of all acceptation, that Christ Jesus came into the world to save sinners; of whom I am chief.
>
> Howbeit for this cause I obtained mercy, that in me first Jesus Christ might shew forth all longsuffering, for a pattern to them which should hereafter believe on him to life everlasting." 1Tim 1:15, 16

> "...shew forth all longsuffering, for a pattern..."

Saul led the persecution against Christ and His disciples. His brutality was well known even in distant cities (Acts 9:13, 26:11). But this was by design for Christ was to make an example of him to the rest of us. Christ demonstrated mercy to a well-known mad man - in order to "shew forth all longsuffering". Show longsuffering to whom? The verse continues: "to them which should hereafter believe on him to life everlasting". Saul's conversion was a public demonstration to the rest of us of Christ's overabounding mercy.

When did the Saul-2-Paul conversion occur? Saul appeared in Acts 7 and was saved in Acts 9. While the exact time is impossible to pinpoint, it was clearly 10+ years before the Hebrew letter was penned. See Gal 2:1.

In his last letter Peter tells us that Christ's longsuffering, written by Paul, was noteworthy.

> The Lord is not slack concerning his promise *[of judgment, 2Pet 3:7]*, as some men count slackness; but is longsuffering to usward, not willing that any should perish, but that all should come to repentance. 2Pet 3:9

> And account that the **longsuffering** of our Lord is **salvation**; even as our beloved brother Paul also according to the wisdom given unto him hath written unto you; 2Pet 3:15

Now, let's contrast what we've learned about Christ's longsuffering toward Saul of Tarsus with a couple of verses in Hebrews. Twice, in Heb 1:13 and Heb 10:12, 13, the Hebrews author referenced Psa 110:1.

> "But this man, after he had offered one sacrifice for sins for ever, sat down on the right hand of God;

> From henceforth expecting till his enemies be made his footstool." Heb 10:12, 13

Thus, after He ascended to heaven and sat down at God's right hand, Christ was "expecting…his enemies" to be judged accordingly ("…slay them before me." Luke 19:27).

But from Paul's letters, coupled with the fact that he himself was the living example of Christ's longsuffering, we know that Christ no longer has that expectation. For at some point in time after His ascension, Christ took an **opposite** course of action in dealing with His enemies. The prophesied wrath was postponed due to God's mercy. First Timothy tells us Christ longsuffered with His enemy by showering Saul of Tarsus with grace and mercy (1Tim 1:14). And this was done as an example to the rest of us. Foreseeable and scripturally-founded judgment was superseded with unexpected and sudden mercy and grace.

So here's the question: Why, at this late date (latter part of Acts), did the Holy Spirit have the Hebrews author write about Christ still "expecting till his enemies be made his footstool" (Heb 10:13)? Note carefully, the word "expecting", Strongs# 1551 (1) is in the present tense (present participle middle in all Greek texts) and (2) is not part of the original verse taken from Psa 110:1. Furthermore, the author does not give any indication or hint to the Partakers in the immediate text that the expectation has been modified, diverted or cancelled – nothing.

Had the Hebrews author not heard of Christ's longsuffering, which was publically and openly demonstrated toward Saul of Tarsus – as a "pattern"? This is quite doubtful, since in the years that had transpired since his conversion, Paul had written several letters regarding God's longsuffering. Furthermore, the Partakers were acquainted with Timothy (Heb 13:23) and even Peter wrote to the "diaspora" that Paul "hath written unto you" regarding God's longsuffering (2Pet 3:9, 15). And according to God's design, many, who had never seen Saul, had heard of his "about face".

> "And was unknown by face unto the churches of Judaea which were in Christ:
>
> But they had heard only, That he which persecuted us in times past now preacheth the faith which once he destroyed." Gal 1:22, 23

Furthermore, as late as Acts 21:24, 25, James maintained there were two groups of believers: a law-keeping group and an "observe no such thing" group. Was Heb 10:13 meant for the ears of one group over the other? And even if it were, it still would not explain why the Holy Spirit chose to write "expecting" in the present tense. Christ was either expecting impending judgment upon His enemies or He was not.

We believe the answer goes back to the wider theme of Hebrews 9 and 10: the emphasis being on the completion of God's prophetic plan for Israel. It was pointed out on page one hundred seventeen that Heb 10:13 was written as the tail end of a sequence of events making up the prophetic plan. It was not written to "update" us on Christ's current attitude toward His enemies. Heb 10:13 was written to affirm that God will judge Christ's enemies. I.E. God is longsuffering now but that does not mean He's forgotten about Deut 18:18, 19 and Acts 3:23. Judgment will occur after God's Mystery among the Gentiles has run its course, giving way for the fulfillment of God's plan for the nation of Israel "as it is written".

Again, we remind our readers that the Partakers were strongly exhorted in Heb 2:1, 3 regarding that "spoken by the Lord". That would include Matt 22:44; Mark 12:36; Luke 20:42, 43 (all in red letters), Acts 2:34, 35 and, of course, Acts 3:23.

Question: Did Paul, formerly the I-obtained-mercy Saul, write Heb 10:13? No one can say absolutely one way or the other, but I find it difficult to believe that Paul would pen Heb 10:12, 13 (using the present tense), while he himself was the poster child for the very opposite action – and in a very public way. Imagine (1) you had been there when Paul wrote Hebrews 10 and (2) you were keenly aware of the Saul-to-Paul conversion story, would Heb 10:13 have confused you? In view of the fact that the Hebrews author was aware of the immaturity of the Partakers (Heb 5:11-13), wouldn't one expect some sort of qualification or explanation to avert further confusion of the already wavering Partakers?

The Antioch Pisidia Sermon

One prominent Biblical author held that Paul's Acts 13 sermon at Antioch Pisidia could

> "...have been spoken by any Jew who had embraced the faith of Christ <u>at</u> or after Pentecost. It is based entirely on the history, and the promises and hopes, of Israel, and upon the coming and work of Christ as recorded in the Gospels..."
>
> *Sir Robert Anderson, Types in Hebrews, page 10, copyright Kregel Publications 1978, reprinted 1981, 1984*

The pronouns "we" and "us" occur six times in Heb 2:1, 3. In order to show no conflict with Paul including himself as part of the "we" and "us", Mr. Anderson emphasized the similarities between Acts 2 and Acts 13. But, the differences between the two sermons speak as loud, if not more so, than the commonalities. Similarities are to be expected. After all, salvation and remission of sins are universal objectives found in all ages. However, differences speak louder because they demand resolution.

An example is taken from my 2nd book (DIED WITH CHRIST); pages 152 through 156. The text below (sandwiched between the bold horizontal lines found below) demonstrates that a seeming similarity on the surface is a big difference after further research.

Let's compare Acts 13:39 (taken from Paul at Antioch Pisidia) with a verse we discussed earlier, Acts 2:44 (Peter at Pentecost).

> "And by him **all that believe are justified** from all things, from which ye could not be justified by the law of Moses." Acts 13:39

> "And **all that believed** were together, and had all things common" Acts 2:44

Many claim that the Pentecostal believers were justified since Acts 2:44 uses the same phrase "**all that believed**" as in Acts 13:39. The thinking goes something like this: Did the people in Acts 2:44 believe? Yes, of course – who can deny it? Then, according to Acts 13:39, they are justified. But closer examination reveals a glaring contradiction.

According to Rom 5:21, those who are righteous (justified) have eternal life

> "That as sin hath reigned unto death, even so might grace reign through righteousness unto eternal life by Jesus Christ our Lord." Rom 5:21

Does that hold true for the saints in Acts 2:44? Refer to Luke 19:12, 13. At Pentecost, Christ had already ascended "to receive for himself a kingdom". Thus, the Pentecostal believers make up the "ten servants" in Christ's parable. Christ is, of course, the "nobleman".

> "He said therefore, A certain nobleman went into a far country to receive for himself a kingdom, and to return. And he called his ten servants, and delivered them ten pounds, and said unto them, Occupy till I come." Luke 19:12, 13

Upon the king's return, each servant was to give an account of how much he had "gained by trading". Rewards and consequences would be administered according to the gain or lack thereof.

The parallel account is found in Matt. 25:14-30, which makes it very clear, that these saints **had to produce** in order to demonstrate their faithfulness. They expressed their faith by their works of obedience. Those not profitable were dealt with eternal severity.

> "And cast ye the unprofitable servant into outer darkness: there shall be weeping and gnashing of teeth." Matt. 25:30

This agrees with the words of Christ in John 15:1-8 when He was preparing the disciples for His absence.

> "Every branch **in me** *(in Christ)* that beareth **not fruit he taketh away**..." John 15:2a
>
> "...the branch cannot bear fruit of itself, except it **abide** in the vine..." John 15:4
>
> "If a man **abide not in me**, he is cast forth as a branch, and is withered; and men gather them, and cast them into the fire, and they are burned." John 15:6

Take note that the unprofitable servant of Matt. 25:30 was included as "**his own** servants" in Matt. 25:14. He was a believer! Since eternal life depended upon bearing or not bearing fruit (being profitable) for the saints of Acts 2:44, we can see they did not have the assurance of eternal life. **The opposite** is true in Eph 1:13, 14 where the believer is sealed (earnest is another word for guarantee) giving the assurance of inheritance and eternal life - see Matt. 19:29b and Titus 3:7.

Accurate Application

So where's the problem? We stated earlier that this was an example of the inaccurate application of certain verses. What is the accurate application? It comes down to differentiating between details and generalities. The question to be asked in both Acts 13:39 and Acts 2:44 is: "believed WHAT?" Believe is a general term and says nothing about what was revealed to the people of Acts 2 or to the people in Acts 13. There is no short cut – the context must be researched and examined to find the answer to the "WHAT?". Let's look at both.

At Pentecost the cross was not presented as good news as found in 1Cor 15:3 – "Christ died for our sins". Rather, in stark contrast, the cross was presented as BAD NEWS. Note the following verses from early Acts:

Acts 2:23 – "**ye**...by wicked hands have crucified and slain:"
Acts 2:36 – "...house of Israel...Jesus, whom **ye** have crucified..."
Acts 3:15 – "**ye**...killed the Prince of life...")
Acts 5:30 – "...whom **ye** slew and hanged on a tree."

Peter, at Pentecost, charged the house of Israel with Christ's murder! Thus, the "what?" of Acts 2:44 was completely void of the cross as the solution to the sin problem. Contrariwise, at Pentecost, the cross was presented as evidence of the sin problem. The reader is encouraged to study early Acts to understand the specifics of the message preached by Peter to Israel.

How about the "what?" of Acts 13:39? Paul was in Antioch Pisidia when he spoke the words of exhortation. This was early in his ministry. However, take note of his letter to Timothy toward the **end** of his ministry regarding this same Antioch.

> "But **thou hast fully known my doctrine**, manner of life, purpose, faith, longsuffering, charity, patience, Persecutions, afflictions, **which came unto me at Antioch**, at Iconium, at Lystra; what persecutions I endured: but out of them all the Lord delivered me." 2Tim 3:10, 11

Timothy was from Lystra or Derbe, which is near Antioch – the greater area of Galatia. Writing to Timothy late in his ministry, Paul stated that his message had been consistent **going all the way back to Acts 13** (Timothy's "starting point"). Since (1) Timothy "hast fully know my doctrine...at Antioch" and (2) Timothy was present when the gospel was first preached in Corinth (2Cor 1:19) and (3) was present when Paul penned the words of 1Cor 15:3, we conclude that the "what?" of Acts 13:39 centered on the cross of Christ as GOOD NEWS. This is quite opposite from the message at Pentecost where Peter presented the cross as BAD NEWS.

All that to say one cannot simply assume that the word "believe[d]" always refers to the same message. We must search the specifics of the message.

In the example above, Matt 25:14-30, Luke 19:11-27 and John 15:1-6 are primary passages which were **"spoken by the Lord"** (Heb 2:3). Any red-letter Bible will illustrate these passages in red font.

These passages are not part of the gospel of the grace of God, which Paul preached.

Scofield Bible

The cover page of the book of Hebrews found in the 1909/1917 Scofield Reference Bible includes the following words in the WRITER section:

> "The authorship of Hebrews has been in controversy from the earliest times. The book is anonymous, but the reference in 2Pet 3:15 seems conclusive that Paul was the writer."

2Pet 3:15 was cited earlier in this chapter and is presented again.

> "And account that the longsuffering of our Lord is salvation; even as our beloved brother Paul also according to the wisdom given unto him hath written unto you;" 2Pet 3:15

Evidently, the "hath written unto you" of 2Pet 3:15 is the reference the author of the cover page was referring to. It helps pacify nagging questions like "if it is not referring to Hebrews, then what happened to those letter(s)?" And, if we do assign it to Paul, it makes things sort of fit. So goes the thinking.

There is a lot of opinion as to which letter(s) Peter is referring to. However, it appears that most commentators favor either Hebrews or 1Ths 4, 5. But a search for "longsuffering" or any of its Greek root word derivatives yields only one occurrence in 1Ths and only two occurrences in Hebrews. And **none** of those three occurrences are speaking about the longsuffering **"of our Lord"**. Rather, it is speaking about the patience of others. See below. The English words bolded in the verses below are translated from the Greek root word: longsuffering.

> "Now we exhort you, brethren, warn them that are unruly, comfort the feebleminded, support the weak, be **patient** toward all men." 1Ths 5:14

"That ye be not slothful, but followers of them who through faith and **patience** inherit the promises." Heb 6:12

"And so, after he **had patiently endured**, he obtained the promise." Heb 6:15

So while, on the surface, 2Pet 3:15 appears to be referring to Hebrews, a casual look in somewhat deeper waters casts doubts on the "seems conclusive" as expressed in the Scofield Bible.

Appendix - The Rest of God

At a recent Bible study, the first question raised about the Rest was "where is it? in heaven? Or on earth?" The answer to this question is not straightforward. Many commentators place it in heaven. Other commentators say it is wherever God is. One commentator said it was salvation. Another said it was the kingdom of God. Very few commentators thought it was on earth. But, you can see from the various answers that each have an element of truth.

First, some technical information: Except for Acts 7:49, all the New Testament occurrences of "rest" (Strongs# 2663) are found in the book of Hebrews. Acts 7:49 is a quote from Isa 66:1, 2. The Hebrew word found in Isa 66:1 is Strongs# 4496. This is the same Hebrew word found in Psalms 95. The text of Hebrews 3 and 4 quotes Psalms 95. All that to say that the Greek word corresponding to Strongs# 2663 in the New Testament aligns consistently to the Hebrew word corresponding to Strongs# 4496 in the Old Testament. One other point to note. Heb 4:9 contains the word rest but it is not Strongs# 2663. It is the word "sabbatismos", which is taken from sabbath.

In looking to answer our initial question, we looked at the immediate text for any light on the subject. Below, we went through each verse in Hebrews and brought out the central meaning as it applied to Rest.

1) "...into my rest" Heb 3:11
2) "...not enter into his rest but to them that believed not" Heb 3:18
3) "...fear...his rest any of you should seem to come short of it" Heb 4:1
4) "For we which have believed do enter into rest...my rest" Heb 4:3
5) "...shall enter into my rest" Heb 4:5
6) "...he that is entered into his rest...ceased from his own works..." Heb 4:10
7) "Let us labour therefore to enter into that rest..." Heb 4:11

Because all New Testament occurrences (with the exception of Acts 7:49) of Rest are found in Hebrews 3 and 4, we need to look at the Old Testament for additional light. Since Hebrews 3 and 4 quote Psa 95, we are back to the equivalent Hebrew word – Strongs# 4496. This word occurs 22 times in the Old Testament. We will limit our examination to this word and to the Rest which David alluded to in Heb 4:7. Since Joshua preceded David by several centuries, it is clear that Canaan was not the ultimate Rest.

A little history is helpful. Shortly after the reigns of David and Solomon, the nation of Israel was divided into Israel and Judah with many kings in each camp. David's reign occurred in approximately 1000 BC. Isaiah lived around 725 BC. By then, each camp was in full rebellion mode. God was sending prophets to each in order to bring His people back; but to no avail. Israel fell around Isaiah's time, leaving only Judah. Jeremiah lived around 600BC. There was a glimmer of hope of national repentance with King Josiah (2Ch 34) but that faded. Around 590 BC, Jerusalem, with its kings, fell to the king of Babylon. According to Daniel 2:34, 35, the final king over the nation of Israel will be Jesus Christ (the stone cut out without hands).

Therefore, to help answer our question, we look in the Old Testament beginning from Psalms. Psalm 132: 13, 14 clearly identifies Zion as His habitation – His Rest.

> "For the LORD hath chosen Zion; he hath desired it for his habitation. This is my rest for ever: here will I dwell; for I have desired it." Psa 132:13, 14

But the same question applies to Zion. Where is it located?

Many Old Testament verses tell us Zion is in Jerusalem (1Ki 8:1; Psa 135:21; Isa 2:3; Zech 8:23; 9:9). But not some heavenly Jerusalem - one located on earth. Joel 3:17 identifies Jerusalem as one where "strangers pass*[ed]* through". Clearly, that could not have occurred in heaven, but on earth as our brief history lesson indicated.

> "So shall ye know that I am the LORD your God dwelling in Zion, my holy mountain: then shall Jerusalem be holy, **and there shall no strangers pass through her anymore.**" Joel 3:17

The verse assures us that strangers will not pass through Jerusalem/Zion as they had in the past.

Isa 52: 1, 2 repeat the same truths.

> "Awake, awake; put on thy strength, O Zion; put on thy beautiful garments, O Jerusalem, the holy city**: for henceforth there shall no more come into thee the uncircumcised and the unclean**.
>
> Shake thyself from the dust; arise, and sit down, O Jerusalem: loose thyself from the bands of thy neck, O captive daughter of Zion." Isa 52:1, 2

When Jesus entered Jerusalem just days before His crucifixion, the book of Matthew described it as such:

> "Tell ye the daughter of Sion, Behold, thy King cometh unto thee, meek, and sitting upon an ass, and a colt the foal of an ass. Matt 21:5

This was a quote from Zech 9:9

> "Rejoice greatly, O daughter of Zion; shout, O daughter of Jerusalem: behold, thy King cometh unto thee: he is just, and having salvation; lowly, and riding upon an ass, and upon a colt the foal of an ass." Zech 9:9

This makes a strong case that Zion and Jerusalem – and therefore God's Rest - were not heavenly but upon the earth.

Quick Glance: Verb Related Definitions

VOICE
    Active voice – subject is doing the action
        Example: John jumped into the pool
    Passive voice – subject is receiving the action
        Example: John was thrown into the pool

MOOD
    Indicative – a statement; an affirmation
    Imperative – a command
    Subjunctive – a supposition; it might occur

TENSE
    Present
    Aorist (with Indicative, it generally means Simple Past)
    Future
    Imperfect – a continuous, ongoing action in the past
        Example: "…they asked of him…" (Acts 1:6) – they just didn't ask one time; they continued to ask
    Perfect – a completed action with present results/impact
        Example: "It is written" (Matt 4:4) – it was written long ago but it still applies today

PERSON

I	We
You, thou	Ye
He, she, it	They

NUMBER
    Singular
    Plural

https://www.blueletterbible.org/help/greekverbs.cfm has a more complete fact sheet on Greek verbs.

Scripture Index

Old Testament

Genesis
  14:18 .... 34, 60
  15:5 107
  15:6 107

Exodus
  12:23 82
  19:1-6 50
  20 131
  20:18 .... 53, 55, 131
  20:19 ...... 53, 55, 56, 131
  24 .... 71, 91, 93, 95
  24:3-8 95
  24:7 95
  24:8 .... 82, 93, 95
  29:12 82
  29:16 82
  29:20 82
  35 92
  35:21 92
  35:31 92

Leviticus
  1-5 111
  4:5-7 82
  4:20 98
  5:10 98
  6:7 98
  14:52 82
  16:14 82
  16:30 98
  17:11 82
  19:22 98

Numbers
  18:22 81
  25 118

Deuteronomy
  6:5 135
  18 .... 44, 132
  18:15 .... 35, 44
  18:15-19 .... 50, 54, 55
  18:16 .... 54, 56, 131
  18:17 .... 54, 56
  18:18 .... 35, 44, 56, 131,
                   133, 140
  18:19 .... 35, 54, 56, 131,
                 132, 133, 140
  27:26 93

1 Kings
  8:1 148

1 Chronicles
  16:16-18 74

Psalms
  2:7 59
  16 18
  95 .... 46, 52, 147
  105:9-11 74
  106:29-31 107
  110 18
  110:1 .... 138, 139
  110:4 .... 34, 61, 64
  132:13 148
  132:14 148
  135:21 148

Isaiah
- 2:3 148
- 52:1 149
- 52:2 149
- 53 84
- 61:7 74
- 61:8 74
- 66:1 147
- 66:2 147

Jeremiah
- 3:13 5
- 24 73
- 24:7 72
- 30 73
- 30:18 91
- 30:22 72
- 31 .... 70, 73, 80, 91, 94
- 31:31 .... 61, 64, 67, 71, 74, 78
- 31:31-34 27
- 31:32 71
- 31:33 .... 72, 100, 117
- 31:34 .... 98, 100, 117
- 31:38 91
- 32 .... 72, 73
- 32:40 .... 74, 78
- 32:41 91
- 32:44 91
- 33 46

Daniel
- 2:34 148
- 2:35 148

Joel
- 2 18
- 3:17 148

New Testament

Matthew
- 4:4 150
- 4:21 102
- 5:48 .... 62, 102
- 10:5 51
- 10:6 51
- 10:22 115
- 13:10 68
- 16:20 68
- 16:21 69
- 16:22 69
- 19:28 51
- 19:29 .... 114, 143
- 20:28 94
- 21:5 149
- 22:44 140
- 23:23 .... 71, 84
- 24:13 .... 106, 115
- 24:47 38
- 25:14 143
- 25:14-30 .... 142, 144
- 25:21 38
- 25:23 38
- 25:30 .... 142, 143
- 26:28 100

Mark
- 9:31 69
- 9:32 69

11:10	51
12:30	135
12:31	135
12:36	140

Luke
2:43	102
9:44	69
9:45	69
12:42	38
18	116
18:9-12	116
18:13	115
18:14	116
18:31-34	69
19:11-27	144
19:12	142
19:13	142
19:17	38
19:19	38
19:27	138
19:40	51
20:36	114
20:42	140
20:43	140
22:30	51
24:25	55
24:26	55
24:44	51, 55, 56
24:45	18

John
1	35
1:21	35
3:34	48
4:22	51
7:40	35
8:26	48
10:1-5	52
10:3	52
10:4	52
10:5	52
12:13	51
14:24	48
14:26	49, 51, 56, 70
15:1-6	144
15:1-8	142
15:2	143
15:4	143
15:6	143
15:15	48
17:4	102
17:8	48, 49
21:25	51

Acts
1:3	18
1:6	150
2	141, 143
2:9-11	15
2:23	110, 143
2:30	68
2:34	140
2:35	140
2:36	68, 110, 143
2:38	69
2:41	15
2:44	141, 142, 143, 144
2:47	15
3	35, 48
3:14	110
3:15	110, 143
3:19-21	77
3:20	77

3:22 .... 35, 50, 55, 56, 68, 132, 133	20:23 21
3:23.. .... 35, 53, 56, 132, 133, 137, 140	20:24 19
3:24 70	21 ....17, 18, 19
4:4 15	21:4 21
4:10 110	21:11 21
4:11 110	21:12 21
4:12 45	21:17 20
5 69	21:18 16
5:14-16 15	21:20 16
5:29-31 69	21:23 18
5:30 .... 110, 143	21:24 ....18, 139
5:31 .... 70, 78	21:25 139
7 138	21:27 16
7:41 118	21:30 20
7:49 147	21:31 20
7:52 110	22:18 ....19, 21
8:30-35 84	24:15 106
9 138	24:18 16
9:13 137	24:23-27 23
11:30 16	26:11 137
12:3 16	26:16 137
13 .... 141, 143, 144	Romans
13:33 59	1:4 ....37, 114
13:39 . 141, 142, 143, 144	3:10 ....5, 106
15 .... 15, 16, 17, 19, 20	3:20 118
15:2 16	3:22 109
15:4 16	3:23 5
15:6 16	3:24 92
15:22 16	3:25 ....92, 98, 100, 122
15:23 .... 16, 21	4:4 118
16 24	4:6-8 ....43, 103
16:1 24	4:13 114
16:4 .... 16, 20	4:16 114
20:16 .... 16, 20	4:25 6
	5:8 ....5, 92
	5:9 92

5:12 5
5:13 43
5:21 142
6 .... 107, 108
6:2 .... 105, 108
6:3 .... 11, 105, 108
6:4 .... 11, 108
6:7 .... 105, 108
6:8 .... 11, 105, 109
6:14 43
6:17 .... 105, 107, 108
6:18 .... 107, 108
6:20 107
6:23 5
7:4 11
7:6 11
8:2 92
8:17 109
8:34 28
9:30 116
10:2 116
10:3 116
10:4 116
11 15
11:6 118
11:25-27 18
13:11 19
13:12 19
15:4 99
15:8 .... 51, 70
15:27 94
16:20 19

1 Corinthians
4:17 19
7:17 19
7:29 19

10:11 99
11:25 28
15:3 143
15:50 103

2 Corinthians
1:19 144
3:6 .... 28, 67
5:20 5
6:2 6

Galatians
1:22 139
1:23 139
2:1 138
2:9 21
2:19 11
2:20 109
3:18 114
3:21 115
3:24 .... 71, 84
3:27 .... 108, 109
3:28 133
4:25 19

Ephesians
1:7 92
1:13 .... 94, 103, 109, 143
1:14 .... 103, 109, 143
2:5 109
2:8 .... 5, 118
2:9 .... 5, 118
4:24 109

Philippians
3:14 .... 76, 77

Colossians
1:14 92
1:26 .... 67, 68
2:20 11

3:1 109
3:3 109

1 Thessalonians
4:15 19
5:14 145

1 Timothy
1:14 139
1:15 137
1:16 137

2 Timothy
3:10 144
3:11 144
3:16 134

Titus
1:5 19
2:11 114
3:7 143

Hebrews
1 49
1:1 49
1:2 ..... 35, 37, 49, 55, 132
1:8 42
1:11 37
1:12 37
1:13 .... 37, 38, 138
1:14 38
2 .... 44, 49, 100
2:1 ..... 38, 49, 51, 70, 77, 96, 134, 140, 141
2:1-4 ...... 16, 38, 104, 110
2:3 ..... 22, 24, 35, 50, 55, 70, 77, 96, 116, 134, 140, 144
2:4 .... 22, 116
2:5 .... 24, 38
2:8 .... 39, 41, 86

2:9 .... 5, 42, 99, 100
2:10 76
2:14 .... 88, 100
2:17 ..... 39, 40, 42, 81, 99, 106, 111, 120
3 .... 44, 45, 46, 147
3:1 .... 24, 31, 51, 76, 77, 104, 147
3:6 106
3:7 .... 35, 52, 55
3:8 45
3:12 .... 123, 127
3:13 .... 31, 120, 123
3:14 106
3:15 .... 35, 52, 55
3:18 147
4:1 .... 123, 147
4:3 147
4:5 147
4:7 .... 35, 52, 55, 148
4:7-11 55
4:9 147
4:10 147
4:11 ..... 55, 100, 111, 124, 147
4:14 .... 32, 51, 99, 121
4:15 .... 80, 99
4:16 .... 44, 80, 121
5 .... 41, 45, 58
5:4 42
5:5 .... 58, 59
5:11 24
5:11-13 140
5:12 .... 23, 24, 116, 123
5:14 102
6 .... 63, 64, 76

6:1	117
6:4	125
6:4-6	124
6:5	125
6:10	24
6:12	146
6:15	146
6:17	59
6:18	24, 59
6:18-20	80
6:20	99
7	60, 62, 63, 64, 80, 91
7:10	63
7:11	61
7:12	61
7:17	81
7:19	60, 62, 81
7:20	63, 81
7:21	62, 63
7:24	81, 99
7:25	40, 62, 81, 99
7:27	88
7:28	63, 75, 76
8	64, 65, 67, 80, 91
8:1	99
8:4	41, 59, 75, 77, 96, 100
8:6	67, 91
8:8	67
8:8-12	94
8:10-12	100
8:12	98
8:13	40, 41, 61, 100
9	65, 80, 83, 91, 140
9:1-10	92
9:7	82, 83
9:8	83, 84
9:9	85, 86
9:11	83, 85
9:11-15	92, 99
9:12	43, 83, 88, 92
9:13	86
9:14	43, 44, 88, 92
9:15	91, 93
9:16-22	92
9:23	95
9:23-28	92
9:24	96
9:25-28	74
9:26	117
9:28	117
10	41, 70, 140
10:1	85, 86, 97, 103
10:1-4	97, 98, 102
10:2	87
10:3	71, 87
10:4	71, 97, 98, 103, 121
10:7	117
10:9	93, 117
10:11	111, 121
10:12	98, 111, 121, 138, 140
10:13	117, 138, 139, 140
10:16	117
10:16-18	117
10:17	117
10:18	33, 117, 122
10:19	40, 96, 112, 121
10:19-23	122
10:21	32
10:22	40, 60, 76
10:23	51, 60, 121, 124
10:24	127

10:25 .... 24, 31, 127	1 Peter
10:26 . 120, 122, 123, 124	1:10 56
10:26-31 124	1:11 56
10:29 .... 120, 122	1:18-20 99
10:32 24	2 Peter
10:32-34 .... 23, 123	3:7 138
10:33 25	3:9 .... 138, 139
10:34 .... 23, 25	3:15 .... 138, 139, 145, 146
11 128	1 John
11:4 107	1:7 44
11:7 107	1:7-9 44
11:13 35	1:9 .... 44, 112
11:13-16 128	1:10 112
11:31 107	3:14 115
12 .... 45, 53, 54, 132	3:15 115
12:1 .... 36, 42, 53, 100, 110, 120	
12:5 .... 25, 31	
12:11 .... 128, 129	
12:18 54	
12:19 35	
12:22 ..... 54, 97, 131, 133	
12:24 .... 91, 97	
12:25 .... 35, 54, 55, 133	
12:26 133	
13:7 25	
13:9 134	
13:15 135	
13:16 135	
13:17 25	
13:19 .... 25, 26	
13:20 .... 74, 135	
13:22 .... 25, 31	
13:23 .... 24, 25, 28, 139	
13:24 .... 23, 25	

www.ingramcontent.com/pod-product-compliance
Lightning Source LLC
LaVergne TN
LVHW010218070526
838199LV00062B/4648